THE JERUSALEM ENTREPRENEUR

BECOMING A SOURCE OF WELL-BEING

"I found the book by Wouter Droppers to be an excellent read! I highly recommend this book. It will help you navigate your faith in your work, which is the *purpose* of our lives. It is a must-read! Many of us businesspersons have questions about how we contribute to the well-being of our employees, vendors, customers, and to our healthy self-interest. How does one balance that in a way that honors God in all that we do? What would Jesus do? This book will assist you in achieving that balance."

—**MARK WHITACRE, PH.D.**, Executive Director,
t-factor of Coca Cola Consolidated Inc., Charlotte, NC

"*The Jerusalem Entrepreneur* is a comprehensive guide for us who are in the marketplace. In the world that we do business in, there are many distractions. However, our best practices and decision-making are to be based on biblical principles. The author, drawing from his extensive experience, demonstrates how we, as marketplace ambassadors, can live an integrated life, pleasing God and bringing values to the people with whom we do business. *The Jerusalem Entrepreneur* is definitely a highly recommended book, showing businesspeople and professionals to be salt and light for the Lord Jesus Christ in this multi-cultural competitive environment."

—**JOSEPH FOO**, Chairman of the board of CBMC-International,
CEO and founder of Jason Marine Group Limited, Singapore

"*The Jerusalem Entrepreneur* provides a desperately needed invitation to let who you are in Christ (identity) change how you do what you do and why. The practical examples and transferable principles could change the game and life of a reader. If more saints in the marketplace lived as Jerusalem entrepreneurs, it would change the world!"

—**MIKE SHARROW**, CEO, C12 Group, San Antonio, Texas, USA

"Every business leader must decide what for them defines success and what they are willing to do to achieve it. Wouter Droppers provides a compelling juxtaposition between worldly success built on selfishness and ambition and godly success built on serving God to the benefit of His greatest treasure—people. By using the biblical narrative of Babylon and Jerusalem, Droppers provides an easy to follow and quite convicting picture of what it looks like to live out of these very different paradigms. Again, every leader must decide what success is and who they will serve in their quest for it, and Droppers helps in this decision with this powerful read."

—**LEE TRUAX**, President, Fellowship of Companies for Christ International

"Successful entrepreneurs all have something in common: a passion for their work. At the same time, this passion is often their pitfall—broken relationships, burn-outs, no money/no rest, and so on. I consider Wouter Droppers to be one of the most inspiring leaders I have been privileged to meet. A brilliant businessman with an unprecedented passion for people. His book, *The Jerusalem Entrepreneur,* is a must-read for every entrepreneur who wants to combine business success with personal well-being."

—**JAN VAN DER VELDEN**, Chairman of the Board of Directors, VDV Concrete & Steel, Belgium

"This book provides a personal testimony of how Jesus Christ is relevant to doing business in these dynamic, challenging times. It is the account of a trial-and-error journey that turns conflicts of interest into healing love for ourselves and others. This book is recommended for anyone looking for purpose and meaning in work and in doing business."

—**PROF. DR. LANS BOVENBERG**, Professor of Relational Economics, Values, and Leadership, Erasmus University, Rotterdam

"I can highly recommend this book by Wouter Droppers. Due to many years in business, Wouter knows who he's dealing with. He knows the tricks of the trade. In this book, he depicts the contrast between two symbolic cities with two business cultures. I was reminded of the first lines of Charles Dickens' *A Tale of Two Cities*.

> It was the best of times, it was the worst of times, it was the age of wisdom, it was the age of foolishness, it was the epoch of belief, it was the epoch of incredulity, it was the season of light, it was the season of darkness, it was the spring of hope, it was the winter of despair...

"We are now experiencing a similar paradox. Which way shall we choose? Wouter gives practical guidance to give this form in entrepreneurship and doing business, in the knowledge that God is the ultimate master builder of the New City."

—**PETER J. BRISCOE**, Cofounder of Europartners and Compass Financial Ministry Europe

"Wouter's book shares valuable experiences from the business trenches that will help the global business community in many senses. It expands on the big 'why' of entrepreneurship from a biblical worldview, it helps with practical perspectives on how to succeed integrally, and it eases the integration of faith and business. Every entrepreneur needs to read it to get real wisdom from a real person who is an authentic, effective, spiritual, and caring leader."

—**DR. JESUS A. SAMPEDRO**, Leadership Author, Program Director/Professor at MACU.edu and CBMC Latin America Chairman

"One field of study often thought to have nothing positive to say about contemporary business is theology. This book demonstrates how misguided this is. In combining his biblical knowledge with his business expertise, the author creates a fresh narrative. It is not only engaging and enlightening but full of practical implications."

—**DR. PETER S. HESLAM**, University of Cambridge,
Director of Faith in Business

"Do Christianity and entrepreneurship affect each other? And if so, how do you manifest this as an entrepreneur? For these questions, Wouter Droppers, in his book, *The Jerusalem Entrepreneur*, lends an excellent helping hand for contemplation and reflection. From the two-opposing biblical images of Babylon and Jerusalem, he elaborates the theme further. I have read this nicely written book with interest and enjoyment and recommend it to anyone interested in learning about entrepreneurship from a biblical perspective."

—**JAN WILLEM OVERWATER**, Former banker (ING),
Current senior boardroom advisor, Netherlands

"Entrepreneurs are important. In the midst of all kinds of forces and influences in our society, they stand for results, continuity, and serving the interests of the stakeholders. How do you do this in a responsible manner, and where are the dangers? In this book, Wouter Droppers contrasts two ways of doing business in a clear and concise manner. One way is destructive, and the other way helps to ensure that entrepreneurs really make a positive contribution to the welfare of society and, therefore, also to themselves. Good to read and useful to reflect on, wherever you are on your entrepreneurial journey."

—**PIETER VAN DER KWAAK**, Chair of the board,
Lansigt Accountants, Netherlands

"With his book, Wouter has made me think in a number of ways. He has made his book wonderfully practical, using countless examples from his own life experience to show how easy it is to make the wrong choices. Navigating between the oh-so-seductive Babylon and the beautiful panorama of Jerusalem requires thinking and fundamental choices. But it is not a distant reality, this Jerusalem. The principles already apply, Wouter argues. Do we dare to use these principles as a mirror for what we do today? For the choices we make, the temptations we are exposed to? Reading this book not only makes you think about things that are sometimes so ordinary but also inspires you to make those conscious choices. Some choices are not difficult (sharpening your company's goals); some choices are incredibly difficult because they are about changing myself and because I have to change some of my ingrained behavior. What Wouter has done with his book is give me an extra mirror by offering me a beautiful and practical reflection on the subject."

—**JAN-WILLEM GRIEVINK**, Christian entrepreneur, Europe

"Daniel was taken by force by the enemies of his people, but he determined not to defile himself, and he had overcome incredible challenges with his firm belief in the Lord. The author challenges all fellow Christian businessmen with Daniel's belief. I think the writer's challenge is the core of Christian businessmen's attitude under prevailing Babylon surroundings. I firmly believe that *The Jerusalem Entrepreneur* can be a most appropriate guideline to today's Christian businessmen and strongly recommend all members worldwide to read and apply for the everlasting success."

—**LEE, DAE SIK**, National Chairman of CBMC, Korea

THE JERUSALEM ENTREPRENEUR

BECOMING A SOURCE OF WELL-BEING

WOUTER DROPPERS

The Jerusalem Entrepreneur
by Wouter Droppers

Printed in the United States of America
ISBN: 978-1-946615-78-7

High Bridge Books titles may be purchased in bulk for educational, business, fund-raising, or sales promotional use. For information, please contact High Bridge Books via www.HighBridgeBooks.com/contact.

Published in Houston, Texas by High Bridge Books.

I dedicate this book to my father, Hendrik Droppers.
He was an example of faith, wisdom, and good entrepreneurship.
I learned much from him.

Arise and shine, for your glory has come,
and the glory of the LORD has risen upon you.
For behold, darkness shall cover the earth,
and thick darkness the peoples;
but the LORD will arise upon you,
and his glory will be seen upon you.
And nations shall come to your light,
and kings to the brightness of your rising.

—Isaiah 60:1-3, about the New Jerusalem

Contents

Word of Thanks

I would like to thank everyone who made this book possible. First, I want to thank all of the people who I have met in my business life. Each of you has—sometimes without knowing it—contributed to the wisdom in this book that I am now able to pass on. You have given me the experiences that have shaped me.

I would also like to thank the Europartners' board, who gave me the time to write this book. Along with Europartners, I want to also thank sponsors Monique and Joost Lensen. You have made the publication of this book possible with your financial contribution.

I would also like to thank the Europartners' team, Annelies Luken and Frans van Santen. Thank you for being the first editors. I appreciate that you put up with me and took the time to constructively criticize my thoughts and words. Thank you both.

I would like to thank all of the readers who read my manuscript and gave their feedback. First of all, I would like to mention my children, Bram Droppers and Marieke Meeske, Nienke Droppers, and Ward Haarsma. Thank you for your input.

And in alphabetical order, I would like to thank the following team of experts: Erik Borgman, Lans Bovenberg, Peter Briscoe, Jan Droppers, Paul van Geest, Gerrit Grievink, Jan Willem Grievink, Gert Hutten, Pieter van der Kwaak, Cees van der Meij, Jan Willem Overwater, Eugene Romijnders, Jan Sterk, Jan van der Velden, and Cors Visser. Thank you especially for your invaluable feedback.

I would like to thank Sarah Berry of High Bridge Media for her advice and editorial work and for making the text flow. I would like to thank Erin van Santen for her translation to English.

Of course, I would like to thank my wife, Elsbeth, who, as is often the case with my projects, has paid a price by seeing less of me, having to listen to my so-called brilliant ideas, or endure my moods on the days I found myself without inspiration to write. She is an angel because, despite everything, she still likes being with me.

Most of all, I would like to thank my Heavenly Father, who is always faithful and who is united to me in his love.

—**Wouter Droppers**
November 2020

Introduction

I once heard an entrepreneur speak about a major reorganization he had carried out. Due to economic circumstances, he had to dismiss 80 employees. He spoke enthusiastically about doing this by email to avoid becoming "emotionally involved." The reorganization was completed quickly and without scruples. Not being emotionally involved was, in his opinion, an asset in making good decisions. It was a quality he was known for.

Not much later, I heard another entrepreneur speak. His business had manufacturing plants on different continents, but he was a modest man who casually remarked that he gave away half of his operating profits to good causes. Later, I heard that he spent a lot of time advising fellow entrepreneurs and employees. Here was a man who was known for serving people and society by sharing his talents, insights, and abilities with others.

These two businesspeople have opposing views of well-being and success. In the business world, I see how entrepreneurs think very differently about being successful. Some entrepreneurs limit their view of success to personal well-being, happiness, and self-gain. They think in terms of power, competition, and winning. Their primary goal is to maximize profit, and their motto is "the end justifies the means." In this book, I call them the Babylonian entrepreneurs, representing the Babylonian business culture.

Others, like the second entrepreneur in our intro, also value the interest of the client and the interest of the other stakeholders. Their primary goal is to improve the well-being of everyone involved, and their motto is "adding value to the client, the society, and the world in an economically profitable way by maximizing the well-being of all stakeholders." These entrepreneurs, when guided in their decisions by God, are what I call Jerusalem entrepreneurs, representing a Jerusalem business culture.

The difference between these ways of thinking about business lies not only in their way of doing business but also in their definition of success and well-being. Success and well-being in the business world are often defined in terms of growth, large profits, a significant income, and a high position in the hierarchy of the company. These definitions seemingly lead to public recognition and the acquisition of desired status symbols. Success is then formed by the prestige you have in society and the rich, abundant lifestyle you can afford. In this way, many business people think they are creating well-being. My personal experience is that this is only a limited truth. I would like to challenge this paradigm of success and reframe the prevailing definition of success and well-being.

The question is this: are we promoting the well-being of the people in this world, including ourselves, or are we creating more discomfort for humans and society by the way we do business? What kind of success are we building with our business and our daily work? Most importantly, *how can we, as entrepreneurs, contribute to the well-being of all of those involved in our company as well as our own healthy self-interest?*[1] This is the question I want to answer.

Changing Perspectives

A great deal of this book reflects my own quest for success, happiness, and well-being, including the uncomfortable side of a strong longing for business success. My life's journey is not yet complete, but the way I define success and well-being has changed. This is equally true for my understanding of the goal of life.

At the beginning of my career, I was motivated by the need for recognition. The opinions of others were of the utmost importance and became my driving force. I began my career by working for a large distributor of spare parts and accessories for passenger cars in the Netherlands. After several successful years working in various management positions, I was asked to become a member of the board of the company, which was an unexpected promotion.

When I took up this position, it was as if I had achieved everything that I could and wanted to achieve. Inside, however, I felt the opposite. I was insecure. Even though this urge to prove myself over and over again had led to good work performance, brought me huge business successes, and brought me onto the board of this company, I felt dissatisfied and empty. My business life was a hunt for recognition and for tangible successes to receive this recognition, but it was without fulfillment and contentment.

Later, I became president of a car dealership with associated companies. The company flourished, we were making good profits, and I was seen as a rising star. Power—and the (ab)use of power—was a new experience. I had never looked at the world from this perspective. As a result, I slowly but surely began to develop egocentric and narcissistic traits. Unbeknownst to me, the world gradually started to revolve purely around me and my ambitions. The attention that success brought transformed into arrogance. People became objects, clients became ATMs, employees became costs, and friends became only a good time. I assessed others based on whether they added value and usefulness to my ambition and goals.

There was a visible and obvious downside to all of this success. I began to live detached from others, arrogant in my own bubble of business success and prestige. Oddly, the downside of it was invisible to me. Only after I saw the tears and disappointment in the eyes of the people I loved in response to my behavior did I realize who I had become. Fortunately, I have a strong and intelligent wife. She began asking me questions about my behavior, motives, and lifestyle choices. I became aware of the dark side of my success and happiness, which was not being interested and connected to others.

In my next job as a president of several dealerships, I learned to think and work in a people-oriented and ethical way. I learned this from a non-Christian entrepreneur, a man of integrity whom I highly respected. He taught me a lot about business ethics. People were his priority. For me, as a task-oriented person, this was difficult. At that time, people were still less important than my business success. I also learned that Christians cannot distinguish themselves from non-Christians by moral values or business ethics. Both believing and non-believing businesspeople can have excellent morals and ethics. Searching for success, happiness, and well-being slowly shifted into questioning. I wondered, *What is the added value of the Christian faith if it's not about ethics and values?*

In 2007, I became president of a movement of Christian businesspeople in the Netherlands called Connecting Businesses and the Marketplace to Christ (CBMC). I had an ambitious business agenda in mind, but something happened to me that had never happened before—I wasn't able to meet the goals I had set for my business performance. That shook me up. Anxiety took over. *How do I explain this? What will people think of me? What will the consequences be?* I decided to go on a retreat to fast and listen to God. It was an unprecedentedly beautiful experience.

During the retreat, I sensed God speaking to me. The first time was from Psalm 127:1-2, where God says:

> Unless the LORD builds the house,
> those who build it labor in vain.
> Unless the LORD watches over the city,
> the watchman stays awake in vain.
> It is in vain that you rise up early
> and go late to rest,
> eating the bread of anxious toil;
> for he gives his beloved sleep.

Those were familiar words. This was *my* life. Up early in the morning, late to bed, lots of hard work with little results. I began to realize that the results were less attainable than I thought and that the outcome and results of my work depended on God's intervention and work. If I did less and God wanted to bless it, the results could be bigger and more abundant than I could predict or imagine. He was in charge of the results, and if God would like to bless me, he could do it, even while I slept.

Three years later in 2010, after the financial crisis, these experiences and the words of Psalm 127 proved themselves true. As a result of my experience at the retreat, CBMC stopped the more expensive activities and concentrated on a limited number of activities designed to change lives. These were less catchy or visible but also required less manpower and financial resources. It was a year with less income, less staff, and fewer activities, but with more business people and entrepreneurs who came to faith. We did less, and God did more. God was visible in our work and present in our daily lives, and that made all the difference. At that point, I remembered the retreat and my lesson from Psalm 127.

The second time God spoke during this retreat was during a reading from Psalm 62:5-9:

> For God alone, O my soul, wait in silence,
> for my hope is from him.
> He only is my rock and my salvation,
> my fortress; I shall not be shaken.
> On God rests my salvation and my glory;
> my mighty rock, my refuge is God.
> Trust in him at all times, O people;
> pour out your heart before him;
> God is a refuge for us.
> Those of low estate are but a breath.

Those of high estate are a delusion;
in the balances, they go up;
they are together lighter than a breath.

This was my second lesson—trust God rather than people. This meant a gigantic change in perspective. Before this change, I feared for my reputation because of my lesser performance. I was afraid of how people would judge me; their judgment was everything to me. I didn't care much about God's perspective on my life. This psalm helped me to put my trust in God. God showed me that his love and presence is enough. He is the only one I can trust and depend on. People and their opinions are not that important at the end of the day. In fact, the psalm calls them but a breath.

However, these revelations didn't mean I experienced nothing but satisfaction and meaning in my work. After five years at CBMC, I was not really enjoying my job anymore. During this time, I dreamed the exact same dream four separate times within one month. In this dream, I was once again working within the last company I had managed during my career in the automotive industry. I wondered what this dream was telling me. Why did I have this dream four times within a month?

In my quiet time with God, when I was looking for an answer, this question came to mind: *How do I view my work at CBMC? Is it a calling or is it an intermediate step toward a more challenging and full life?* When this question was raised, I knew the answer. My role was to bring entrepreneurs and business people to God and to mobilize Christian entrepreneurs to be ambassadors for Christ. My life story and work experience had prepared me to fill this role. After this realization, I found joy in my work again. I felt meaning and fulfillment again. I would not return to the business world for my own ambition or new challenges but would continue to serve and lead others.

I continued to serve at CBMC for several years until I felt that God was nudging me in a new direction. The board of

Europartners,[2] a European movement of business leaders, considered my experience in serving a ministry for business leaders in the Netherlands and my business background quite valuable and invited me to become their new president. I accepted this invitation and have been working with Europartners for many years now. In this role, I help Christian business leaders intentionally live out the gospel and non-believing business leaders come to Christ. During these years with Europartners, I am discovering more and more what it means to live by grace.

I live from a deep awareness that life is greater than my abilities. In my current work, I am learning to receive and be thankful. I am more and more aware of the fact that God gives everything in advance. We can only use and live from what God has given first. As an entrepreneur and human being, I am grateful for what I have received and can work with. It is my privilege to make God's outpouring of gifts fruitful by blessing people. Achieved results do not just come from my own efforts—it is God who is at work through me and is capable of blessing my work regardless of my own actions. After my work, I give my effort back to God in the knowledge and trust that he wants to work through it, using my work in his way to honor and serve him.

The challenge nowadays is to work from the knowledge that God is the master builder of the new city and the new world. Although this knowledge should give space and freedom, it can be hard for me to hand over control and live from what God is giving. Trusting God is still a struggle. Working from the knowledge that God is always willing to start over again and that failure is an opportunity to grow gives me hope and encourages perseverance. Although I know this, I still listen too much to the opinion and judgment of people. Too often, that is truer to me than God's truth. I continuously need to internalize that truth so I can work from the conviction that God is always there. When I do this, I can work with confidence, knowing I am secure in his love. This is the main thing that keeps me going. Whatever happens or whatever I feel, he will be there to take care of me because he loves me. His love will never fail. It is secured in him, and not in my performance.

My definition of success and well-being has changed. Previously, I worked hard for business success, money, and reputation. This gave me all kinds of status symbols, which yielded a sense of being respected and loved. Now, I define success, as becoming the person God wants me to be, and well-being, as being able to live from grace.

My life goal has changed from pursuing success, wealth, and respect for myself to becoming the person God wants me to be. This implies living the kind of life that Christ lived, trusting God, living from what He is giving, and bringing God's kingdom and future to earth in my daily life. It is important to me that the people around me can flourish and blossom since God desires this for them. This changed perspective and the lessons I learned I hope to impart to you through this book.

What is this book about?

Throughout this book, we will reframe the terms of success and well-being in business by answering this question: *"How can we as entrepreneurs contribute to the well-being of those involved in our company and our healthy self-interest?"*[3]

I will focus on entrepreneurship from a perspective of calling and purpose, discussing how we can do business out of love for all stakeholders of the company by serving them well and with excellence. Together, we will discover how this perspective can contribute to a better world while giving us as entrepreneurs more joy and meaning.

How do we begin? By looking at two symbolic cities in the Bible: Babylon, the city of people, and Jerusalem, the city of God. In my own search, I drew lessons from the history of these two cities and applied them to entrepreneurship and businesses. If we can understand the origins and principles of both cities, then we can recognize them in people, in leadership, and in how we do business today.

Before We Begin

If I'm talking about the entrepreneur, I'm talking about female and male entrepreneurs. However, for simplicity's sake, I will refer to the entrepreneur as he. In addition, there is sometimes a broader concept that includes the businessman/woman, director, executive CEO, and the professional. I will not continue to mention all of these titles separately, but in most cases, they will be included in the term "entrepreneur." A characteristic of each of these people is that they are empowered to make decisions and are responsible for both the profit and losses of the company or departments within the company while having the freedom to operate as an entrepreneur.

In this book, I distinguish various types of entrepreneurs.

First, I discuss the Babylon entrepreneur, who has a Babylon worldview and lives and works according to Babylon values.

Second, I explain the Jerusalem entrepreneur, who has a Jerusalem worldview and works according to Jerusalem values. I will explain the terms Jerusalem and Babylon in the first part of the book.

Third, I note the Christian Jerusalem entrepreneur who has submitted his life to Christ as Lord. The Christian Jerusalem entrepreneur in its true sense embraces Jerusalem values and dedicates his finances, possessions, company, and life to Christ as Lord. A good friend once gave me the following definition:

> A Christian Jerusalem entrepreneur is someone who is called and equipped with talent, character, and personality traits to co-create with God in the world of business for the greater good, God's righteousness, and God's glory.

We will work with this definition in the second and third parts of the book.

Finally, the practical examples in this book are all true stories. To protect the identities of those who are mentioned, I have adapted the stories by changing the industry, the size of the company, the country, the name, or my relationship with the entrepreneur. I hope that as you read these stories, you will identify with or relate to an aspect of each story in your own life, encouraging you to apply God's definition of success to your own circumstances and relationships.

Section 1

The Tale of Two Cities: Babylon and Jerusalem

1

Two Cities: Babylon and Jerusalem

Welcome to Babylon and Jerusalem, two cities with opposing views, cultures, and spiritual powers. Babylon is the city of people, which tries to be powerful, eternal, godly, and unforgettable. Jerusalem is the city of God, which is eternal. God's city is a true representation of well-being and will always be visited and remembered because of God's presence and wisdom. In Babylon, the people try to play the role of god, are obsessed with power, and are addicted to kicks, wealth, money, status, glamor, and worldly success. The people in the other city seek to serve God, his people, and others out of love for righteousness and justice.

The historical city of Babel or Babylon is an ancient city that, according to the Bible, was established by Nimrod, who was a mighty hunter and a mighty warrior.[1] He was the first on earth to exercise power in order to dominate people and build his own kingdom at the expense of others. Today, we would call him a megalomaniac since he was obsessed with power. He established a strong and powerful kingdom in the Middle East. He built Babylon and other big cities like Nineveh, Uruk, Akkad, and Kalneh.

Babylon was already an important and significant city in his days. It soon became the capital city of Babylonia, a kingdom in ancient Mesopotamia that lasted from the 18th to the 6th centuries BC. But it reached the height of its fame as the predominant city of the growing Babylonian kingdom in 626-539 BC. Under King Nebuchadnezzar (605-562 BC), it became one of the most beautiful cities of antiquity. The city became famous for its hanging gardens, one of the seven wonders of the world. Under the rule of Alexander the Great, Babylon flourished as a center of study and trade, but after his death in 323 BC, the kingdom was divided among his generals. So began decades of change and strife, with Babylon at the center of it all. The ongoing insurrections laid waste to the once-thriving city. The remains of the city are in present-day Hillah, Babil Governorate, and Iraq, about 85 kilometers (53 mi) south of Baghdad. [2]

Like Babylon, Jerusalem is an old city. Jerusalem is one of the 20 oldest inhabited cities in the world. It was an ancient Canaanite city, formerly called Salem.[3] Jerusalem is located in Israel on a plateau in the Judaean Mountains between the Mediterranean and the Dead Sea. Jerusalem reached its fame under King David and King Solomon. It was the capital of the United Kingdom of Israel. Solomon built a temple for God in Jerusalem, and this was the place God filled with his glory where he dwelled among his people.

In 589 BC, the city and temple were destroyed by Nebuchadnezzar of Babylon. For a moment, it looked like the city of Babylon was stronger than Jerusalem, but Jerusalem was rebuilt. Throughout its long history, Jerusalem has been destroyed at least twice, besieged 23 times, captured and recaptured 44 times, and attacked 52 times, but it still exists.[4] In the Bible, these cities appear to be opposites in every respect. Babylon is a symbol for the city of people, people who want to be god and independent of God. Instead of listening to God, the people of Babylon follow their own desires and insights. They think they are free but don't recognize that they are under a spiritual power that is guiding and forming their desires and ambitions. The book of Revelation calls this power the great prostitute of Babylon. Jerusalem is a symbol for the city of the God who became man. The inhabitants of Jerusalem desire to live from what God is giving. They are willing to turn away from their own opinions, insights, and efforts and turn to God, the source of life, good, love, and righteousness.

The Spiritual Power Behind Babylon

In chapters 17 and 18 of the book of Revelation, we learn that the prostitute of Babylon is the spiritual power behind Babylon. She represents warped values and principles, like her love for gold, precious stones, pearls, outward beauty, and abominable things. She hates the people of God and she is seen *as the mother of the abominations of the earth.*[5]

She is an invisible power that can influence our emotions, our thinking, and, thus, our actions. Her power has a specific and interesting characteristic: when we, as humans, refuse to make choices and withstand it, it grows to rule over us. Her power extends to the ends of the earth. "The woman that you saw is the great city that has dominion over the kings of the earth" (Rev. 17:18).

Her motto is "I sit as a queen, I am no widow, and mourning I shall never see."[6] She is proud, narcissistic, and loves only herself. When she reveals herself in people, they say things like, "Me first, my business first, and my people and nation first." She uses her abundance of wealth and power to profile herself as a benefactor. But when the appearance of doing good endangers her real agenda, her benevolence comes to a full stop and she is willing to break her vows.

She will give anything to be successful in her pursuit of power, personal happiness, and wealth. She represents the shameless exploitation of the vulnerable, grasping for unlimited self-fulfillment at the expense of others. She has created her own norm. She says, "I decide what's good. And what's good for me is good for everyone else." There is nothing outside of her self-created norm. She does what she wants to do and indulges herself in the name of freedom. She has become her own god. The person who adopts this lifestyle is worshipping none other than the prostitute of Babylon.

The lifestyle and culture she's promoting are not foreign to us—we see her power and influence around us every day.

Babylon's religion is wealth, hedonism, unlimited personal freedom, and self-fulfillment. We can see this clearly in the business world, in politics, and in the worldviews and actions of ordinary people. As humans, we are all influenced by her. She is a part of us. If we do nothing, she will make us hers.

Humanity Objectified

One driven by Babylon's worldview sees fellow people as a threat to his own well-being and prosperity. Others are simply competitors. Control, power, scarcity, and fear determine the Babylonian way of thinking. People become dehumanized as they are sized up as commodities, obstacles, or threats. In the prostitute of Babylon's worldview, a human being without value can easily be imprisoned or disposed of. She ensures that people see each other as objects to be used for desire and pleasure. She presents one to the other within the lens of egocentric personal ambition. People see each other as utilitarian objects, not as an equal human being with intrinsic value.

From the very beginning, the Bible is clear about how God values man; he is an image-bearer of God and the crowning jewel of creation.[7] When man lays down this original value or when it is taken away from him, he loses his identity. He then becomes no higher than creation itself. Man may be smarter and more intelligent than animals, but he doesn't naturally distinguish himself from them. The prostitute of Babylon makes man an object to satisfy her egocentric self-interest. Civilization is no longer judged by its humanity and care for the individual marginalized man as God judges it[8] but by its power, wealth, and technological progress. Man's value is determined by his economic contribution to society. If man no longer has economic value, he is deemed worthless. He has forgotten his God-given identity.

Suffering is foolish.

In Babylon, purpose and meaning are centered on personal well-being and individual happiness. Everything is determined by self-interest and economic worth. Suffering for something bigger than yourself seems like insanity or foolishness. Instant gratification takes precedence over long-term good for others because personal pleasure is the greater good and it must happen now. The idea that doing good—like service, compassion, and mercy—comes at a price is foolishness. Living and doing business is no longer about serving others but about negotiating and claiming as much as you can for yourself.

Babylon's Allure

For centuries, kings, rulers, and ordinary people have wanted a piece of the luxurious, decadent lifestyle that the prostitute of Babylon possesses and exudes. The people and nations of this earth allow themselves to be seduced by her, like a man seduced by a beautiful woman. They want to experience her lust. They like to be in her house full of luxury and wealth. They indulge in her hedonistic lifestyle. Business people, entrepreneurs, and large corporations have long been fond of her. They do good business with the money she spends on luxury items. Everything is extravagant—the best money can buy.

The city of Babylon flourishes and grows through its culture of consumption and spending power. Everyone is seduced by the promise of more. They are seemingly unable to ignore the glittering attraction of the here and now rather than the less flashy but more substantial growth of a society motivated by the good for all. That is why she is called the great prostitute. The people are prepared to push down their real convictions to be part of this life of status, wealth, and pleasure.

The culture of Babylon represents selfishness and narcissism. The goals are beauty, prestige, and wealth, and the point is to enjoy it at all costs. People are instruments to achieve goals, and people's very lives are an acceptable price to pay for pleasure. Everything about Babylon is designed to lure and entrap. In doing so, the culture of Babylon seduces and controls those in power: business people, nations, and entire cultures. And it also wants to seduce you and me.

The (New) Jerusalem

In stark contrast to the narcissistic city of Babylon, Jerusalem is the city of God, the place where God dwells and rules.[9] Jerusalem, as we know it from both biblical and secular history, is the physical predecessor of the New Jerusalem named in Revelation chapters 21 and 22. This New Jerusalem is named after this city because God used the earthly Jerusalem to establish his name on earth and dwell there. This will be the city that will last forever.[10] The New Jerusalem refers to the meaning of the earthly Jerusalem. The earthly Jerusalem points toward the future. The past and future belong together and point to each other.

God wants us to love and serve as he does and requires man to actively choose. God makes himself available to help us in this, but he doesn't push or force himself on humanity. God is currently enthroned in heaven but also lives on earth through the presence of the Holy Spirit. By the Holy Spirit, God is also present in people who believe in Jesus.[11] The New Jerusalem is a still-hidden city, only revealed in the future as the bride of Christ.[12] The city symbolizes the Body of Christ, where the Holy Spirit lives.[13] The New Jerusalem is something of the future and of the present, with the future beginning now and still arriving until it is finally and fully revealed in the days ahead.

In the book of Revelation, the New Jerusalem is called the bride of the Lamb (which is imagery for Jesus).[14] The image of a bride is used because it symbolizes a loving relationship between a husband and wife, partners who are willing to sacrifice themselves for the other. God gives his glory and splendor to this city and binds himself to it. This spiritual power doesn't put itself center stage, nor is it obsessed with its own beauty and glory, but instead, it cares about humanity. God becomes man in order to serve man. He dresses the city, his beloved bride, beautifully with gemstones and beautiful clothes. The inhabitants of the city find their happiness and well-being in the presence of Jesus and God the Father. Their deepest longing, being together, is fulfilled.

The beauty with which God builds the city is not the outward beauty or accumulated prosperity of Babylon but the beauty of the inner self.[15] God's character and personality become visible, giving the city its glory and appearance. The beauty of the city lies in its love, joy, peace, patience, kindness, goodness, faithfulness, gentleness, and self-control.[16] The Holy Spirit gives the beauty of the Father and Jesus to the people. The clothes of the people in this city are made of pure, radiant linen, which represents the good deeds of those who belong to Christ.[17]

The gems adorn the city and its foundation. These gems are God's promises made available to all people by Jesus, as proclaimed by the apostles. This proclamation can be summarized by this statement: "God loves to share his glory and majesty and his '*being*' with people." He likes to be present in them to share his being, character, personality, and values with them. In other words, the outer beauty of the city finds its origin in what God is creating on the inside of his people. This is symbolized by the foundation of this city, which is also decorated with gems, although they are below the surface. The beauty of the city is in people—people who are bought by Jesus and merged with God, where *being* (inside) and *doing* (outside) coincide—people who are whole and true to God's image and likeness.

The city flows with justice, peace, grace, restoration, abundance, and love. Its citizens experience a deep sense of well-being. They are home. Death, mourning, lamentation, and pain no longer exist. God is wiping away every tear.[18] No one thinks about the past; no one is lured by the beauty of Babylon or desires its return.[19] People have nothing more to fear; oppression is a distant memory, and they are able to live in freedom.[20] The city is alive, and it is there to bless those surrounding it.[21] Nations come to it to receive wisdom and insight and to honor God. Its gates are always open.[22]

Defined by Love

The New Jerusalem is defined by the love in its relationships and in its servant posture. After all, the New Jerusalem is about a bride and groom. It is about a God who lets go of his position and wants to live among his people and take care of them.[23] It is about Jesus, who was willing to die for the victory over evil and sin. It is about a God who allows his beloved Son to be a sacrifice in order to demonstrate the fullness of his love for us.[24] This love is a part of God's being; love is inextricably linked to who he is.

To be more specific, it is the love described in 1 Corinthians 13:[25]

> Love is patient and kind; love does not envy or boast; it is not arrogant or rude. It does not insist on its own way; it is not irritable or resentful; it does not rejoice at wrongdoing, but rejoices with the truth. Love bears all things, believes all things, hopes all things, endures all things."

The word *love* here has a deeper meaning than erotic or romantic love. There are different kinds of love. These can be best explained by the four Greek words used to define love.[26]

1. *Eros* is an erotic, sexual love. We won't focus on this type of love in this book.
2. *Philia* is the kind of love between friends that is mutually reciprocated. We speak mostly about

this type of love in the chapter "Love in Business."

3. *Storge* is about natural love and affection, the kind that small children receive from their parents. Without this kind of love, children would not grow and thrive. This kind of love, which characterizes God, teaches us to share and forces us out of ourselves. We will make sacrifices to nurture this kind of love.

4. *Agape* is about loving the whole person. This love is an inner source that flows from within and is shared and given away. It is the love for the whole of creation and God, which includes ourselves and our fellow human beings.[27] It is the love that can give without expecting anything in return. It is this love that God gives and wants to be the source of our thinking and existence. *Agape* is the central theme beyond all principles and laws God has given to man.[28] He desires that this love will determine our behavior and actions.

These last two forms of love are characteristic of who God is.

Justice

The city of God is founded on justice,[29] as revealed by the message and the good news of the disciples.[30] The word *justice* has several facets. The first is a legal aspect. When someone commits an offense, he or she receives due punishment. When possible, they must pay for the damage they caused the victim. In a fair trial, legal justice is done on behalf of the victim.

justice = legal + restoration
term

The second facet of justice is restoration. Once justice is served and the punishment is given, the restoration aspect focuses on restoring the identity and relationships of the perpetrator. After paying the penalty and expressing regret, there should be room for people to regain their places in society. In this way, man is allowed to start functioning again, just as he is intended to within society.

A beautiful example of this kind of justice is the Truth and Reconciliation Commission (TRC) in South Africa, which came about after apartheid. Chaired by Anglican Archbishop Desmond Tutu under the leadership of President Nelson Mandela, the TRC chose to restore the country by repairing relationships. Those harmed or victimized by apartheid were given a public apology by President Mandela on behalf of the state and allotted conciliatory funds. Some perpetrators were given amnesty for apologizing for their crimes. The TRC worked hard to emphasize reconciliation and recovery over punishment and retaliation.

In the New Jerusalem, God delivers his own kind of justice to humanity. Humanity is restored to its original purpose as image-bearer of God and ruler/king over creation. Justice is done to the poor and oppressed by restoring and raising them up.[31] Justice is served to the rich and the proud by returning them to their origins as people who live by the grace of God.[32] There will be a general reset wherein the enemies of God, the wicked and evildoers, receive their punishment and the righteous, humble, poor, and weak who call for help will be saved.[33] People receive a fair and honest trial, and no judgment is given based on appearance or based on rumors. Jesus remains true to his values and his promises.[34]

The New Jerusalem is characterized by the Jewish word for peace, *shalom*. Evil is gone; the destructive forces have been conquered and destroyed. There is no more struggle. *Shalom* expresses more than simply the absence of war. The word means security, rest, and peace of mind. The meaning of shalom encompasses an abundant life, a deep sense of well-being, and the idea of coming home. *Shalom* is a blossoming, the process of becoming who you are and how you were made to be.[35] In the New Jerusalem, we discover who we were truly meant to be.

Babylon's Start: Nimrod's Power

In returning to Babylon, we're reminded of the city's ancient roots, with the first stories of its settlement originating in the biblical book of Genesis.[36] The city was established by Nimrod, history's first great conqueror on earth[37] and the first recorded megalomaniac and tyrant.[38] He is the first recorded ruler who expanded his kingdom by using power to conquer and kill for glory and self-preservation. Flavius Josephus said, "Nimrod gradually changed the government into tyranny."[39]

Before Nimrod, it was not the norm to use power in this way to build empires. In the tribal and family culture of that time, the use of power to conquer, to subjugate others, and to become a single great and powerful entity was unheard of. Certainly, wars were waged over water sources, land, or as revenge on an alleged injustice, as well as for evil reasons,[40] but the founding of cities and the building of a "world empire" by means of power, violence, and warfare, was new for the time.[41] The Bible calls Nimrod the first one who did this.

At that time, people mostly used their power to care for one another. Well-being was not about the self but about the community. Talents, skills, and opportunities were used to take care of one another and to add value to the means of living. Care for the land yielded bigger harvests, and care for the animals made the animals fat, made them strong, and increased the production of milk and offspring. Care for the family made the family strong and resilient. Good stewardship paid off in higher yields, more prosperity, and welfare for all. Care and attention, with added value through honest work, nurtured prosperity, and health.

Nimrod seems to be the first to challenge this paradigm of caring for the means of existence as a welfare model, using power to hunt, beat, and kill for personal gain as a model for prosperity and welfare. Nimrod was a hunter; he killed and he took. He did not add value to the source of living; he used it and killed it. The cost of Nimrod's way of life is scarcity and the destruction of countless lives. Multiplying and prosperity are replaced by death, struggle, competition, and victory.

Our reality today is much more civilized and restrained, often with a system of laws, checks, and balances. Yet in today's business world, I still see these two prominently distinctive thoughts, dating back to the time I have just described, that guide business leaders. These two distinctive thoughts are:

1. We grow our business and create prosperity and well-being for our stakeholders by taking care of them and by adding value (the original form of multiplication and the creation of well-being).
2. We grow as a company and become richer by eliminating competition; we are egocentric in the ways we do business in order to increase our market share (the Nimrod paradigm).

In my experience, these two forms are often intermingled. Sometimes business leaders deliberately try to bring someone down by creating alternative facts or even by using private detectives to gather information about competing leaders. At the same time, these leaders work on the improvement of their business by innovations and by adding value to the customer with better service and higher performance. Let me give you an example from my personal business experience a long time ago. When I was president of a company, we decided to make the client our top priority. We intentionally looked for ways to serve the client and other stakeholders better.

I remember the moment I was celebrating our number one position in the market share reports. However, this achievement was not primarily because of our own performance—it was because of the poor performance and failure of our competitors. I discovered in my heart that I was celebrating their failure and downfall instead of our own success and improvement. There was much of Babylon in my own heart even though I had tried hard to create Jerusalem values. All of us live in the tension between Babylon and Jerusalem, drawn to both cultures.

The Tower of Babel[42]

In Nimrod's Babylon, the people decided to build a monument for themselves, shifting the focus from God to man. The Babylonians said, "Let's build a city with a tower that reaches into the sky; that will make us famous, and then we won't get scattered all over the world."[43] There are three elements to this story:

- In building a tower that reached into the sky, man demonstrated his desire to become God, to inflate his sense of self-worth, and find his own way to heaven.
- In his idea that the tower would make him famous, man revealed his demand to be independent of God.
- In his determination not to be scattered, man showed his compulsion to live alongside others in order to feel safe and powerful. Trusting God was replaced by a self-made sense of power and security.

In his hubris and efforts to construct something bigger than God, man sidestepped his identity of being created in God's image and tried to *become* God. His identity as the crowning creature was no longer enough; he wanted power and dominion. God refused to let this happen. He confused the speech of the people, bringing their project to a halt.

God saw what the people were doing because he himself had created them. God made humanity incredibly intelligent,[44] the ruler of creation, a fact that makes man unprecedentedly powerful. But this turned into a curse when destructive, evil spiritual powers started to control and lead him. Nimrod's power, one with the paradigm of killing and conquering, and an identity that is both separate from God and needs constant affirmation, was an extremely dangerous cocktail for man.

God understood that man's indomitable power and might in Babylon would lead to destruction if given free rein. By confusing their speech, he prevented this power from coming to fruition early in history. If we look at the construction of the tower of Babel, we see that the city fell apart because of God's interference.

Jerusalem's Start: Melchizedek

Babel is held in stark contrast to Jerusalem. This is equally true for its leaders. Nimrod, the first king of Babylon, is the complete opposite of Melchizedek, the first known king of Jerusalem. In his time, Jerusalem was called Salem,[45] the city of peace. The name Melchizedek means "the king of justice and peace." Pointing to Jesus as the true king of justice and peace, Melchizedek offered a different way of establishing a city.[46]

What's interesting about Melchizedek is that he was a priest as well as a king. As the priest of the Most High God, he was the one who blessed Abraham,[47] one of the greatest patriarchs of his time[48] and a father of the faith.[49] Like God with Abraham, Melchizedek takes a position of blessing. He wants to bless rather than conquer like Nimrod. He is also a king of justice and peace. He wants people to come into their own, to flourish and grow, in contrast to Nimrod, the great human killer and exploiter.

As Christian Jerusalem entrepreneurs, we are leaders equipped to bring justice and peace. We are also called to bless others and be priests who proclaim and exalt God. As Peter writes, "But you are a chosen race, a royal priesthood, a holy nation, a people for his own possession, that you may proclaim the excellencies of him who called you out of darkness into his marvelous light."[50] This implies that we as entrepreneurs are not only working toward the well-being of people but also for reconciliation and proclamation. We have a special position as envoys and priests of God. Paul confirms this when he writes,

> All this is from God, who through Christ reconciled us to himself and gave us the ministry of reconciliation [...] therefore, we are ambassadors for Christ, God making his appeal through us. We implore you on behalf of Christ, be reconciled to God.[51]

This task is a calling for all those who have committed themselves to Christ.[52] All Christian entrepreneurs, therefore, are also priests and ambassadors of Christ. Through the example of Melchizedek, we see that our task as Christian Jerusalem entrepreneurs is twofold: to bless people through our leadership and to proclaim and exalt God through our behavior, work, and speech.

Babylon's Ending: The Great Downfall

Babel's brick tower, created to make a name for the people of the city, ended up abandoned as its people reacted in confusion over the new languages they began to speak to one another; they "dispersed over the face of the whole earth."[53] The prideful tower resulted in the city's ultimate downfall. This downfall of Babel is one of the earliest biblical stories, found in Genesis 11, and it prevented man from exercising his full power to create life according to the Babylonian values and to control earth.

One of the last biblical stories, in Revelation, details Babylon's final hours. These passages give us remarkable insight into the last days of the great prostitute of Babylon, where she is ruling almost the whole world with her power and doctrine. Only

God and his people are withstanding her; therefore, she hates them and persecutes them. We learn that she controls and reigns over the great kings of the earth and all people.[54] But when the countries and empires she rules[55] finally realize who she truly is, they bring her to ruin and leave her naked. This end comes suddenly and is accompanied by deadly plagues—disease, mourning, famine, and annihilation—which will strike her in one day.[56] All that she has worked for vanishes in an instant. We are even told that her wealth and prosperity evaporate within one hour.[57] The fall of Lehmann in 2008 is child's play in comparison to what will happen in the future. Whatever Babylon occupies, along with its culture and economy, will disappear forever.[58]

Babylon's attractiveness and promises of short-term gratification are dazzling. She is stunning and sells herself well. But she doesn't see her end coming. Who do we put our trust in? The power of Babylon is strong, and with this power and its values, we can build great kingdoms, businesses, and prestigious companies, but they will be wiped away suddenly. They will neither last nor have eternal value.

The Completion of Jerusalem: Becoming the New Jerusalem

The final act of the Prostitute of Babylon ends in destruction. Jerusalem does not end; rather, it is the eternal city of peace. It is a blessing to the world and all its inhabitants for all eternity because of God's presence and promises.[59] The Bible calls this renewed and recreated city the New Jerusalem, the city of God's people, who belong to Christ.

What is the New Jerusalem?

This city, the New Jerusalem, is actually a group of people who belong to God. They have committed themselves to Jesus as their Savior and Lord. Together, they are his bride. In a way, the New

Jerusalem is already present on earth today through the lives of committed Christians who love Jesus. This community of God's people and Jesus's followers will be revealed in its full glory in the future.[60] Today, it is a broken vessel with a precious treasure inside, which is Christ, the Son of Man.[61]

The New Jerusalem is Christ's "community," and Christian entrepreneurs who have submitted their lives to Him are part of it. The hallmark of this entrepreneur is that he wants to live, think, and work in unity with Jesus out of love for him. This unity is transforming him from the inside out. It is changing his desires and longings and, therefore, his actions and behavior, which are all about God's vision for this world and humanity.

God's Vision for This World

God's vision for this world is visualized in Isaiah 65:

> "For behold, I create new heavens
> and a new earth,
> and the former things shall not be remembered or
> come into mind.
> But be glad and rejoice forever
> in that which I create;
> for behold, I create Jerusalem to be a joy,
> and her people to be a gladness.
> I will rejoice in Jerusalem
> and be glad in my people;
> no more shall be heard in it the sound of weeping
> and the cry of distress.
> No more shall there be in it
> an infant who lives but a few days,
> or an old man who does not fill out his days,
> for the young man shall die a hundred years old,
> and the sinner a hundred years old shall be accursed.

They shall build houses and inhabit them;
they shall plant vineyards and eat their fruit.
They shall not build and another inhabit;
they shall not plant and another eat;
for like the days of a tree shall the days of my people be, and my chosen shall long enjoy the work of their hands.
They shall not labor in vain
or bear children for calamity,
for they shall be the offspring of the blessed of the Lord, and their descendants with them.
Before they call I will answer;
while they are yet speaking I will hear.
The wolf and the lamb shall graze together;
the lion shall eat straw like the ox,
and dust shall be the serpent's food.
They shall not hurt or destroy
in all my holy mountain,"
says the Lord. (Isa. 65:17-25)

This world of God and our future is the inspiration of the Christian Jerusalem entrepreneur. It drives his actions and behavior. Out of his love for God and humanity, the Christian entrepreneur strives for righteousness and works for a world where everything is according to God's righteousness. The Christian Jerusalem entrepreneur can, therefore, be described as *someone who is called and equipped with talent, character, and personality traits to co-create with God in the world of business for the greater good, God's righteousness, and God's glory.*

An example of a Christian entrepreneur is Barry. He runs a company in construction and roadbuilding. He is doing business with many different governments and municipalities in various nations. He serves the people of these nations and contributes to their well-being by using his skills clearly and visibly—improving the way of living and economy by improving their infrastructure. In addition, he appointed chaplains to take care of the personal and spiritual well-being of his staff. He also developed a task force within the company for fast and immediate help in areas where catastrophes take place. Finally, a large amount of his profits goes to the company's trust, which finances all kinds of charities. If you asked Barry what motivates him in his work, he would not tell you about how great the company is but, rather, what it does for people and this world. He considers his company to be a source for good and a tool to serve humanity. In this way, he is co-creating with God.

One day, the head of a particular government was corrupt and wanted to take bribes, but Barry was not willing to pay them. Because of this behavior, he was missing orders, but over time, the admiration of this corrupt government official started to grow. After a while, this government official became severely ill and did not know what to do. He was afraid of losing his life and family.

One day, he visited Barry in his office and pointed toward the Bible on his desk. He said, "Could you lend me your Bible? I would like to read it." He openly shared about his illness and life. He admitted to taking bribes and, therefore, was not able to give orders to my friend, although he liked him more and trusted him more than his competitors. His longing for money and wealth always superseded his sympathy for Barry. He asked Barry to pray for him because he knew that Barry was a believer.

Barry prayed for him, gave him the Bible, and now they are developing a friendship. Barry said, "I was always angry with this guy because he was corrupt, but now I have discovered that he is God's present to me. It is a privilege to be part of what God is doing in this man's life." Barry received more satisfaction from what happened during this meeting than money could ever give him.

Which kind of life do you want? Which city and which culture do you want to make your point of departure and your ultimate home?

2

Doing Business in a Babylonian Culture

If, as entrepreneurs, we choose to settle in Jerusalem, how can we live and work in a business environment with Babylonian qualities? The life of Daniel gives us important principles for a Jerusalem entrepreneur within a Babylonian culture. Daniel is a perfect example because, as an exile from Jerusalem, he lived in an entirely Babylonian culture where the God of Jerusalem was no longer tangible or visibly present. In fact, in the competition between Babylon and Jerusalem, God seemed to have lost. From a human point of view, Babylon controlled Jerusalem at this time. Everything that was of value to the believers from Jerusalem was sacrificed and dedicated to the god of Babylon.[1]

Daniel's Example

Daniel was seen as a young man with great potential. As a trainee, he was extremely talented and gifted. He lived in a time similar to ours—God was viewed as no longer important or not even present.[2] Daniel was taken by force by the enemies of his people, the Babylonians, and found himself serving a hostile government. This enemy had destroyed Daniel's country and deported its people. Someone working for an enemy government after a hostile takeover that has destroyed one's homeland is called a traitor in most cultures. Nevertheless, Daniel served it with all his might and ability.

In the first chapter of Daniel, we see Daniel tested for the first time about the matter of food and healthy nutrition. As one of the new trainees, Daniel had to look impeccably healthy. All the trainees were put on a tight schedule of eating, exercising, studying, and resting. The food was the same food that the advisors prescribed for the king's meals, rich food of excellent quality. Daniel asked his supervisor to deviate from the rules and serve him and his friends a strict diet of vegetables and water. That was quite a request. It may have sounded like a stubborn and inherently disrespectful response to being offered the best food in the kingdom. His manager was also afraid that if he granted Daniel's request against the king's orders, he would lose his position or maybe even his life.

Daniel proposed a trial period as a test to determine which food led to the best results. For ten days, he and his friends ate only vegetables, while the others ate the king's food. At the end of the ten days, he and his friends looked healthier and fitter than everyone else. His convictions compelled him to go against the predominant culture surrounding him.

He received a high position, became the ruler of the most important region in the empire, and also became the head of all the country's advisors and wise men.[3] Among these sages were the magicians, conjurers, and fortunetellers who were despised by the religious leaders of the exiled Jews. Moreover, these were the people God warned about in his Torah, the law.[4] They were involved with dark, spiritual forces and were not looking to God for salvation.

Through displaying an incredible amount of courage based on confidence in his God, Daniel later joined the top of the government and was even considered for an appointment over the whole kingdom, along with two other government officials.[5] This Daniel, probably seen by some of his fellow countrymen as a traitor and corrupt individual, was used to establish God's name within the realm of Babylon.

The king of the Babylonian empire, the great Nebuchadnezzar, humbled himself and accepted God as his king[6] because Daniel showed him who God is. Daniel then served King Darius in the Persian Empire. The effect of this ministry was that Darius commanded everyone in the great Persian empire to show respectful awe for God.[7] Daniel's position and his understanding of his ministry and calling had a great influence on the realm he served.

Daniel's Secret

How did Daniel not only survive as a "Jerusalem man" in this Babylonian culture but also go on to become one of the most important people in that kingdom? How did Daniel become an instrument of God, well-known and respected within Babylonian culture? How did Daniel become a person of blessing in that great empire? What was Daniel's secret? I suggest that his secret can be reduced to just one decision that determined his whole life and future. In the book of Daniel, it's just a single sentence. Daniel's choice was this: "But Daniel determined that he would not defile himself."[8] In other words, Daniel was firm in his resolution to obey God's commandments. Often unrecognized as a crucial and decisive moment for everything that takes place in a person's life, this choice determines what one's life will become.

This decision changed everything. Daniel chose not to be swept along with Babylon's cultural values; he decided to remain faithful to God. Determinedly, he made a decision with his heart. God, therefore, used him to share his words and insights. This made Daniel a blessing for his bosses, for the people of Israel, and for the great empires of Babylon and (later) Persia. This decision, which was anchored in his heart, allowed him to resist the many temptations of culture. This choice was crucial.

Imagine you are scouted by a large multinational cooperation. They see that you have great potential and are very gifted. You receive a traineeship and have the chance for an extraordinary career, even with the possibility to become president or CEO. You no longer introduce yourself with only your own name but with a mention of your position and company. People want to be seen with you and your status grows.

No matter where in the world you go, this is your status; everything is at your fingertips. The only catch? You have to stick to the precedents and culture of this company. The company's rules and culture are not necessarily bad or wrong—they are just different from the personal values and beliefs with which you have been raised. In the market within which a business operates, to grow or die is the order of the day. Internally, this is also the culture: you participate and grow, or you disappear. Anything is allowed. What do you do?

Daniel faced his own dilemma when he was asked to integrate into the Babylonian culture through eating its food. He risked his life and the lives of his friends by saying no. How did he handle this? He searched for ways to achieve his desired goals that fit within his convictions.

Daniel's Strategy

Daniel didn't leave, he didn't resist, he didn't invoke his rights, he didn't sue anyone, and he wasn't the morality police or a whistleblower. What did he do? He thought of an alternative action plan.

This requires wisdom, among other skills. These are the very things in the business world that you can't learn at school. Alternative action plans require conviction, innovative thinking, and God's help. They don't automatically lead to a success story, yet they provide a chance. In many businesses, the culture says that *the end justifies the means*. This is often abused, but the motto also offers unprecedented opportunities and possibilities. For us as Christian professionals, the challenge is to implement this motto positively. From it, we can develop and introduce alternative methods to the cultural norm. Our challenge is to show that there is a better way of doing business.

Daniel hadn't yet built up his credentials or proven himself, yet he dared to take a stand. He ignored the group pressure that undoubtedly existed. Fully aware of the competition among these trainees, Daniel dared to be different. Most of us know from our own experiences how difficult that is. To show individuality in this phase of being unknown is admirable and commands respect.

Values and Truthfulness

Good and healthy leadership is characterized by two things: the leader's values and the leader's truthfulness. At crucial moments, great leaders can make the right choice based on their own values, contrary to the usual culture and established conventions. Consider Gandhi, Mandela, Martin Luther King, Jr., William Wilberforce, and others. All of these leaders had difficulties in battle. Many times, progress was slow and uncertain. But their vision, their driving force, was greater than the personal suffering they had to endure. In the story above, Daniel had a clear strategy:[9]

- He trusted God and was devoted to God in prayer.
- He persevered in making his decisions with his heart.
- He had clear values.
- He was willing to take risks and stick his neck out.
- He asked instead of demanding.

- He understood the interests of all stakeholders and those of his executives.
- He had concrete alternative proposals and plans.

Are these easy to apply in every situation? Do they always lead to desired business success? Definitely not. But they do lead to a beautiful and attractive life, full of adventure and unique experiences that call for courage and risk.

Another example is Bilal, the entrepreneur of a small enterprise, who came to the Christian faith within a Muslim community. In the evening, he regularly receives threatening phone calls. His intimidators try to make it impossible for him to do business, but he remains faithful, continuing to live where he lives. He is convinced his calling is to be a witness to Christ within that community. When he was asked how he kept this up, he answered in his strong-accented English, "God is good." That is his faith and conviction and, therefore, is the end of the conversation. Life is not always easy for those who live out their beliefs and ideals, but it is worth it.

Jesus is the supreme example of being truthful. He was one of a kind in every aspect of his life. His thinking, being, acting, feeling, and speaking were all connected and voiced the same message. Jesus was willing to die for his values and what he believed. His love for humanity and this world was not only a virtue. Jesus was the embodiment of love. Therefore, he was able and willing to give his life for humanity and this world. For Jesus, love as the highest virtue was non-debatable, because it is who he is. If he gave up love, he would be denying himself. It was precisely this act of love that exalted Jesus and caused God to give him a name that is above all names.[10]

A Life Above Reproach

We all have to deal with jealousy and resistance when our "star is rising." Daniel experienced this himself when the king considered appointing him to lead the entire kingdom.[11] The other leaders became jealous and tried to overthrow Daniel. They couldn't find anything, however, to accuse him of.

The only weak point was his faith in the God of Jerusalem. This brings us to something that should define us as Christians in business: living a life above reproach. Imagine what that would do to our image! A friend once told me that in a certain district in his country riddled with corruption, the mayor gives preference to civil servants with a Christian background because he knows from experience that they do not allow themselves to be bribed.

Daniel's reputation preceded him, and he responded to the jealousy of the Babylonian leaders by changing *nothing*. Although it had become illegal to pray to anyone but the Babylonian king, Daniel resumed his prayers to God, fully aware of the new law he was breaking. As he prayed on his knees to God for salvation, he was arrested, and despite having the king's favor, was thrown into a den of lions.

Courage and Trust

We can't rely on our own integrity or reputation to save us. Daniel's clean track record didn't help him, and he ended up in the lion's den, though God eventually saved him from it.[12] Living above reproach doesn't guarantee a problem-free life. Certain people are determined to see us as the enemy and bring us down. I've heard stories of people hiring private detectives, blackmailing employees, instigating fake news, inciting rumors, and using other tactics to reach their goal.

Within business life too, these Babylonian business tactics are used when major interests are at stake. Unfortunately, the person who wins is often openly admired, even if he "won" by illegal means. In the Babylonian culture only the winner counts. While living in a kingdom full of influential people who used selfish tactics, Daniel showed his allegiance to his Jerusalem citizenship by keeping his focus and continuing to trust God. His trust shows us that we, as Christian Jerusalem entrepreneurs, can also do things in a countercultural way.

It reminds me of Will's story.[13] Will was running his own production company when his right-hand man, John, suddenly resigned. Will had invested a lot in John and hoped he would become his successor. The relationship was more than just business—Will and John were friends and equal business partners. Will was completely taken aback by John's announcement that he wanted to leave the business. His disappointment deepened when he found out that John had started his own company in the meantime. He had copied their best-selling product and had become Will's main competition.

Nine years later, John had a design problem with one of his new products. Partly as a result of this, several lawsuits threatened to ruin his business. Meanwhile, Will had forgiven John and prayed for him regularly. During one of his prayers, he felt strongly that God was telling him to help John. Will decided to buy one of John's products and discovered where the design problem lay. He commissioned his engineers to solve the problem, and after several modifications, he called John to show him where the problem was.

Will trusted that God would help him. Some would say this was radical Christianity. Others would say this was stupidity. Only time will tell how John will respond to this act of unconditional, Christ-like love. The results are not Will's responsibility. His responsibility, like ours, is to do what the Lord wants him to do. Will reacted out of his trust in and understanding of God and not out of envy, fear, or resentment. He shows what it means to be a real Christian entrepreneur.

Another example of an entrepreneur trusting God and doing business in a countercultural way is Henk, a great entrepreneur in the construction industry. I had just arrived for a visit at Henk's house when I saw a local contractor, who had recently become bankrupt, leave Henk's home. When I asked him about this, he said, "Oh, I helped him with a loan so he could start over." I was surprised and asked him, "Why would you help a competitor restart his business?" Henk replied, "I think I have to do this, and we have to remember that God can give us more than both you and I could ever earn."

Henk exemplified what Peter said when he wrote, "Keep your conduct among the Gentiles honorable, so that when they speak against you as evildoers, they may see your good deeds and glorify God on the day of visitation."[14] This is how we define our beliefs and live out our choices. What is more important—our status, as being a successful entrepreneur, and our company or our beliefs and our testimony?

In addition to trusting God, two truths play a role in being able to endure injustice and can help us respond well to various situations.

The first perspective is this: at a certain point, God's justice will be done. Our job is to trust. This helps us endure injustice and continue to do good.

The second perspective is this: God is there. He wants to help us endure suffering for the greater good that is to come.

> For this is a gracious thing, when, mindful of God, one endures sorrows while suffering unjustly. For what credit is it if, when you sin and are beaten for it, you endure? But if when you do good and suffer for it you endure, this is a gracious thing in the sight of God.[15]

Commissioned to Bless

Earlier in this book, in describing Melchizedek as king of Jerusalem, we have seen that he is a king who wants to bless. Even for those who live in a Babylonian culture, blessing is a calling. God gives clear instructions to Daniel and the people of Israel about how they should live in the Babylonian exile. Jeremiah writes a letter to the exiles in the name of God:

> Thus says the Lord of hosts, the God of Israel, to all the exiles whom I have sent into exile from Jerusalem to Babylon: Build houses and live in them; plant gardens and eat their produce. Take wives and have sons and daughters; take wives for your sons, and give your daughters in marriage, that they may bear sons and daughters; multiply there, and do not decrease. But seek the welfare of the city where I have sent you into exile, and pray to the Lord on its behalf, for in its welfare you will find your welfare.[16]

God wants to make himself known to the world. He is focused on our well-being and not on our misfortune. He would like to restore our fortunes.[17] God's compassion for all people must guide our attitude. God calls for an active attitude to bless and be a blessing for the city and its inhabitants. We see this with Melchizedek,[18] and we hear Jeremiah encouraging the people in exile to practice this.[19] More importantly, Jesus calls us to do good[20] and use our talents[21] for the people,[22] and we see it in God's behavior as Lord of the New Jerusalem.[23]

God wants to save. We are called to be a blessing and to make Christ and the New Jerusalem visible on earth. In the Sermon on the Mount, Jesus says:

> You are the light of the world. A city set on a hill cannot be hidden. Nor do people light a lamp and put it under a basket, but on a stand, and it gives light to all in the house. In the same way, let your light shine before others, so that they may see your good works and give glory to your Father who is in heaven.[24]

God wants us to enter the world and influence it with his good way of thinking. It is the love of Christ that sets us in motion and drives us to bless the world and its people with our presence and our actions.

Section 2

The Christian Jerusalem Entrepreneur

3

Who Are We?

In this section, I am giving extensive attention to the question, "Who are we as entrepreneurs?" All our acts come out of who we are, how we think, what we long for, and what we believe about this world. Together, this shapes our behavior in life and in business.

In Babylon, man sees himself as the sole possessor of his life. "I" is considered the highest authority. This *I* is autonomous, independent, and not accountable. *I* considers himself his own god. The qualitative difference between *I* and the other is determined by personality, appearance, and performance. His identity as an entrepreneur lies in his performance and how others experience him. Self-realization, success, and performance are of the utmost importance. A successful life must be created and curated by the entrepreneur. Therefore, the entrepreneur is responsible for his own success and happiness.

However, being created in God's image means that man himself has intrinsic value. Because of this, he does not have to prove his economic worth. A person's life is valuable in itself because God created him in his own image and likeness to experience a relationship with God himself. This is what distinguishes man from the other visible beings in creation. God's glory shines in man. He wants to share himself, his greatness, and his glory with man. Humanity is very precious to God. He thinks about us; he made us and loves us unconditionally.

The entrepreneur who thinks through the lens of the Jerusalem perspective sees himself as a created being. He knows he is wanted and loved. He is created with a purpose and destination; he wants to serve others and depends upon and is accountable to God. His identity lies in his existence as a human being in relation to God. In the New Jerusalem, God is deeply involved with man and is very present in his life. That which is built is not humanity's own paradise but the kind of world God has intended to come to fulfillment — a world built on the foundation of love and righteousness. The people and entrepreneurs who live in Jerusalem do not find their lives' purposes and successes within themselves but in something larger than themselves.

Role and Identity

Too often, we confuse our *identity* with our *role* in society. "We are not what we do, we are not what we have, we are not what others think of us," priest and writer Henri Nouwen[1] once stated.[2] To believe the opposite makes one's identity, performance, and position in a society dependent on the appreciation of others. This belief system[3] imposes conditions on who I am; I am only somebody if I am successful, earn a large paycheck, wear the right clothes, am a good employee, a good partner, or a good lover. However, this way of thinking interprets me not as a human being who simply is, but someone fabricated by my performance, position, or behavior, making me dependent on my environment for my worth. I then need to continuously adapt myself to my surroundings and adjust to its feedback. Putting on an identity determined by my environment doesn't allow me to explore who I truly am but imposes conditions on who I must become. And the messages in that kind of environment are constantly changing.

A Rooted Identity

A rooted identity drawn from a worldview rooted in healthy values tells me that I am known and loved. Like the root system of a tree, this sense of self keeps me secure, making sure I'm not blown away by strong winds. Knowing I am known and loved is important for both a rooted identity that takes a stand when life is against me and one that doesn't run away with me if I am deemed successful.

Being known means that someone else knows me completely, including all my failures and successes. He or she knows when I am ashamed or when I feel guilty, as well as when I am proud or feel victorious. He or she knows my strengths and weaknesses, my insecurities and talents, but loves me completely nonetheless. I then feel safe and can be my whole self with him or her without playing a role. It is a place that I can call my home. For me, this home is God. He knows me completely, he loves me, and he poured out his life for me. I never have to feel ashamed and guilty because he knew me before I was born. Even when I was his enemy, he took the initiative to draw me into his presence and love.

Someone else who knows me very well is my wife. With her, I don't have to pretend or perform to receive her love. Therefore, I can be myself completely and love her freely. This is important for a rooted identity.

Being loved means knowing God loves you and that other people do too, in all of your strengths and weaknesses. This kind of love wants you to be purified from what is unhealthy with respect to personal freedom and individuality. Because love includes an element of respect, love is limited in its effectiveness as a change agent. Love requires active participation; it does not force or coerce. Nor does love justify what is distorted or evil. It doesn't manipulate or control. Love is invitational, seeking connection, wanting to give itself. Love asks and then listens for an answer. Love is the root of all existence, creating a community focused on the good of all. It doesn't change because of the circumstances; the circumstances change because of it. Love is a crucial ingredient of a rooted identity.[4] And it requires vulnerability.

The combination of being known and being loved and being able to know and love others contributes to a healthy identity development. You can just be. You don't have to hide. Shortcomings don't directly equate to failure. Because of this, there is no shame and no condemnation—only growth. Experiences, behavioral patterns, and character traits may be made visible in order to be able to see, discover, discuss, and develop them. In this way, you grow toward your fullest self and away from self-condemnation. In addition, by being open and vulnerable, you also get to know others more easily, which contributes to a stronger identity. When we can consistently live in this identity, we are better able to serve others from the places we are gifted with a sense of calling.

Vision and Values

Our calling and desire to follow Jesus determines our vision and values and, therefore, our course in life. These are hallmark qualities of the Christian Jerusalem entrepreneur. If we use the metaphor of a ship, vision is like the rudder; it determines the course toward our ultimate destination of knowing and being known. The values are like the keel or underside of the ship, which makes sure the ship doesn't capsize. Values give stability. Without values, we are guided by what works now regardless of whether it's right. Values anchor us and make us reliable. Values determine the quality of life and how we want to live it. Vision not only has to do with the end result we are aiming for but also how we want to achieve our goals as entrepreneurs. Finding your vision and goals in values and "guiding principles" is evidence of wisdom. It allows you to stand your ground in all circumstances. In our rapidly changing society, vision gives the entrepreneur stability and helps him make choices. The trick is to stick to your vision and values, even in difficult times. They are life's guiding principles.

I once spoke to Linda, an entrepreneur who had been appointed over a conglomerate of businesses in trouble. The board of directors feared bankruptcy. Everyone advised Linda to sell or restructure the failing businesses and lay off 10% of the employees. That would send a "strong signal" to the banks, shareholders, and suppliers. The first year would mean losses, but it would provide a stable and healthy basis to build back up to good and healthy profit figures in subsequent years. Linda chose not to do this. Her reasons?

1. She didn't want to fire people whose skills she later needed again.
2. She knew that the market was changing and that a good distribution network would give her a crucial advantage.
3. She believed in the business, the market, and herself.

What to do? Linda decided to keep her head down and stake the first year on her reputation as a skilled and professional leader who was able to grow businesses and make them profitable. This was a gutsy decision in which she put her own position and reputation at risk. Her personal values were that people are important and entrepreneurship makes people flourish and businesses grow. This vision regularly brought Linda into conflict with the board of directors, the shareholders, and the banks in both the first and second years she was with the company. The company wasn't recovering fast enough for them.

Despite the odds, Linda stayed the course because she knew she had a rooted identity and a clear vision. Linda knew who she was; she was not dependent on others nor was she dependent on success. She wanted the business to flourish based on her values and not based on a heartless quick fix. Linda succeeded. She was the hero and the great inspirational leader with whom everyone wanted to do business. It could also have gone differently. Linda knew this but still chose this daring path to do business based on her values.

Along with being known and loved, vision and values determine the outcome and quality of our existence. The quality is based on which culture we worship—Babylon or Jerusalem.

Essential Characteristics

A Christian entrepreneur who is motivated by the values of Jerusalem differs from his secular colleagues in that he knows he is called by God. He is inspired and driven by the values of the New Jerusalem and God's kingdom, and he wants God to guide his entrepreneurship.

A Christian Jerusalem entrepreneur has many essential characteristics that follow out of our aforementioned definition: *"A Christian Jerusalem entrepreneur is someone who is called and equipped with talent, character, and personality traits to co-create with God in the world of business for the greater good, God's righteousness, and God's glory."*

- His work is more than ambition or a form of personal self-development (Chapter 4). He is called and sees his work and entrepreneurship as calling.
- He wants a connected life. He knows how to connect with God, his neighbor, himself, the world, and his ideals (Chapters 5, 6, and 7).
- He has received the qualities to start and run a business. He's excited and ready to shoulder the responsibility that this brings (Chapter 8).

- The fruit of his entrepreneurship is righteousness. He wants to do justice to people, God, and creation so that everything may be in its rightful place as intended by God (Chapter 9).
- Everything is about the well-being of people and the glory of God. This is where he finds his motivation and where he experiences meaning (Chapters 9 and 10).

The following stories show how the source of your identity determines the outcome and quality of your life and business.

The Stories of Two Entrepreneurs

Can an entrepreneur who calls himself a Christian get stuck worshipping the vision and values within the Babylonian culture? I think so. To illustrate, I'm going to share the stories of two entrepreneurs, Jim and Marc. Jim is an example of a Babylonian entrepreneur who calls himself a Christian. Here is Jim's story. Jim bought a farm in a country that was not yet very developed economically. He wanted to give shape to his Christian identity by doing something good for the people there. Moreover, he thought it would be good for the image of his European company and himself.

Jim saw entrepreneurship as his identity, which meant his success as an entrepreneur was crucial. He saw his faith as an obstacle to being able to do business full-on. Calling himself a Christian too often conflicted with his clever Babylonian business instincts. He was proud of himself when he made smart deals that were just within the confines of the law. This law, not the Jerusalem-based law, turned out to be the ethical framework of his faith. By appealing to the letter of the law, he could justify even unethical actions.

So Jim bought an overseas company from a good friend and colleague. The payment took place over three years. With this, Jim hoped to keep sufficient liquidity. He expected and hoped that the purchase, through growth, efficiency, improvement, and new markets, would pay for itself in this three-year period. He saw sufficient opportunities. But soon, Jim encountered all kinds of unexpected financial setbacks.

The experienced manager, who could not cope with the dominant style of leadership of his new boss, left. He found Jim's dominant style of leadership humiliating.

Full of resentment, the manager tried to turn the local population against the business and Jim, which caused lots of problems. Jim had trouble finding employees who wanted to work on his farm. Machines broke down that couldn't be repaired. The irrigation system sometimes didn't work for weeks.

Soon, Jim discovered that he couldn't transfer hard currency from this country to his European bank account, which meant he couldn't take the potential profit out of the country. In short, the purchase of the new company that should have contributed to his Christian image and identity turned out to be a disaster. Jim felt deceived and refused to pay the last two installments of the purchase price. The case became a lawsuit, and everyone involved talked about what a shame it was.

The second story is about an entrepreneur named Marc, who is an example of a Christian Jerusalem entrepreneur. Marc found his identity in God and embraced the Jerusalem values. Marc also bought a farm abroad, but he did it to help the local population find work and food. He planned to use the profits to invest in schools, hospitals, and the area's economic development. Problems arose when his manager was discovered trying to take over the business. He began to blackmail Marc using his position, power, and local influence.

Marc began praying. He asked God whether he should withdraw and sell the business or continue. He sensed God telling him to keep going—that he would have difficult years, but he must continue to invest. He traveled regularly to his company for a year to talk to the people, assisting them, training them, and helping to give them a vision for the future. He even brought other entrepreneurs to the country and taught them the culture.

After one year, Marc decided to give the manager half of his company and put an end to the drama. With the other half, he continued independently. From this part of the company, he built a new flourishing farm. The other entrepreneurs also founded businesses and the region began flourishing economically. Together, they invested in hospitals and schools. They built wells and started children's sponsorship projects. Marc's dream was realized.

If we break down the stories and take a closer look at what happened, we see that Jim's focus became his own image and identity as a successful entrepreneur. His role had become his identity. He depended on what others thought of him instead of having a rooted identity of being loved and known in which performance doesn't matter. Next to that, he didn't internalize and embrace the values and vision of God in his heart. He maybe didn't even realize that he was slowly taking on and reinforcing this Babylonian trait.

Because his identity was on the line, success became crucial. "I cannot fail." This became his driving force instead of the Jerusalem value of focusing on the good and well-being of all involved. His addiction to success and his fear of what failure would do to his image pushed him to take measures that could be called unethical, although technically within the confines of the law.

Jim began to be even proud of this ability to cheat the system. His leadership style was domineering (after all, it was *his* identity on the line). Instead of using his leadership gifting to connect and inspire, he alienated his employees and found that many of the local population had turned against him. Faced with the loss of the thing he desired the most, a successful image, instead of reconciliation, Jim looked for retribution, which ended in a lawsuit and a loss for both sides. Too often, the Babylonian culture promises a glittering image and delivers brokenness for everyone involved.

Marc, on the other hand, began with a vision bigger than himself: to help the local population by investing in the area's economic development. Marc knew that he was loved by God and could, therefore, carry his role as an entrepreneur lightly. His identity and role did not merge. Because Marc knew he was loved by God, he had no need to prove himself. This meant he could leave all circumstances to God. He sought gratification in what God gave rather than his own performance.

Marc also experienced setbacks and problems, just as Jim did. He even found himself with enemies. However, Marc's Jerusalem culture showed when Marc prayed and begged God to show him what to do. He set aside his short-term gains for long-term investment. This included giving away half of his company to his competition, someone who had hurt him, because it would benefit the community in the long run. After all, this had always been Marc's long-term goal. Slowly, Marc's dream began to be realized. Two entrepreneurs, two identities, two different outcomes. The source of our identity determines the quality and outcome of our life and business.

4

One Who Is Called

Being aware of one's calling is the first characteristic of the Christian Jerusalem entrepreneur. His work is much more than pure ambition or a form of personal self-development.[1] The Christian Jerusalem entrepreneur knows he is created by God with a purpose and a calling, including caring for creation and the people God has entrusted to him. He is called to be steadfast, to be responsible, to show integrity, and to show compassion. The good kings of Jerusalem realized they were only stewards of the real king, who is God.

A perfect example of a king who realizes his calling as God's servant is when God asked Solomon, "What I shall give you?" Solomon answered, "Give your servant an understanding mind to govern your people, that I may discern between good and evil."[2] Solomon knew that he had been appointed king over what was already God's. He felt a responsibility to guide God's people and was trying to live out his calling for something bigger than himself.

Babylon represents a human culture that says, "I am my own god and I do what I want to do." The calling of the Babylon culture is centered on self-realization, personal glory, pursuing happiness, and avoiding pain, as is embodied in the great prostitute of Babylon. Her motto is, "I sit here as a queen. I am untouchable. I want to be full of glamor and indulgence." Her calling comes from within herself.

Why is it important to have a calling?

"He who has a 'why' to live for, can endure almost any 'how,'"[3] wrote Viktor Frankl.[4]

A calling is the Christian term for living with a purpose. A calling is more than just a purpose because it is put on one's heart by God. We don't just live here for ourselves; we are here for a reason. When you can internalize this reason and make it to your personal *why*, you have found your calling as a Christian. A calling gives your life purpose and meaning. It provides a reason to live and get out of bed every morning. It drives your behavior and actions, and it defines how you look at this world. Without a calling and a purpose bigger than yourself, you become the center of your life and will easily slip into the Babylonian culture.

From the Bible, I distinguish six universal callings or vocations.

Six Vocations

We often hear the words "calling" and "vocation" used interchangeably. In Latin, the word vocation literally means calling, and originally referred to men and women who had chosen a monastic life, living apart from the rest of society. Martin Luther expanded the term, applying it to men, women, and children in ordinary life and in ordinary work. Vocation isn't limited to *what* we do but includes also *how* we do it. A vocation answers the *why* question and defines the *how* and *what* questions; therefore, it is of utmost importance to understand your vocation. Otherwise, you can and probably will miss the full life God has in mind for you; you may end up somewhere you don't want to be. In the Bible, we see six separate vocations. The starting point and the basis for the first four vocations can be found in the Bible's explanation of creation. God creates man for a reason, and he gives man a task within creation.

> Then God said, "Let us make man in our image, after our likeness. And let them have dominion over the fish of the sea and over the birds of the heavens and over the livestock and over all the earth and over every creeping thing that creeps on the earth." So God created man in his own image, in the image of God he created him; male and female he created them. And God blessed them. And God said to them, "Be fruitful and multiply and fill the earth and subdue it, and have dominion over the fish of the sea and over the birds of the heavens and over every living thing that moves on the earth."[5]

> The Lord God took the man and put him in the garden of Eden to work it and keep it.[6]

In these passages, we can see the first four vocations. The first is to be an image-bearer—to be a human in God's image and likeness. The second is to have dominion as a servant leader. The third is to be fruitful and multiply. What is our heritage, and what is our legacy?

The fourth vocation stems from two core principles that remain relevant no matter how society changes. These principles are summarized by Jesus: "So whatever you wish that others would do to you, do also to them, for this is the Law and the Prophets..."[7] and "You shall love the Lord your God with all your heart and with all your soul and with all your mind... And a second is like it: You shall love your neighbor as yourself."[8] So the fourth vocation is to love God and others as we love ourselves.

The fifth vocation is to serve in a specific place or position.

All of these vocations hinge on the sixth one: living in connection and unity with God and Christ.[9] Without a connection or understanding of who God is and how he works in our lives, we will fail when trying to live out the first five vocations in our own strength. God's deepest desire is that we would be in a relationship with him and that, from that relationship, we would be able to love and serve God and others in our daily tasks and professional responsibilities.

It is important to recognize that all these callings are described with verbs. In no way are they dependent on a certain job position, successful outcome, or on how respected our work is by others. Vocations are possible in every situation and in every believer. They exist in the very ways in which we shape our lives and our work. John Piper says, "You don't waste your life by 'what' you do, but by 'how' and 'why.'"[10] The heart matters more than the job description. Let's take a closer look at these vocations in the context of the New Testament and our daily work.

1. Being God's Image-Bearer on Earth

Bearing God's image on this earth is an incredible position to be in. We are encouraged to create and work, and we have the freedom to do this in our own way. We don't do this in isolation but are part of a greater whole: God and creation. Being God's image-bearer should give us a deep sense of meaning and responsibility. But what does it really look like to carry the image of God within us? An image-bearer is made up of three parts, which we will look at more closely below.

Creating

In the kingdom of God, God wants us to create in freedom. This allows us to express our ideas, our feelings, our ways of thinking, our character, and our personalities. As entrepreneurs, we dream and have plans and ideas. We would like to realize our dreams by creating. God took five days to create an environment in which man could flourish. Every single day of creation ended with the refrain, "And God saw that it was good." In this way, we as entrepreneurs can also be present in a creative way to create an environment for man to thrive. When we do this, we are actually doing what God did. He dreamed about you and this world and is in the process of realizing his ideas and dreams.[11] We are free to work and walk through life with this same creative bent.[12]

Reconciled to God

Being God's image-bearer on earth gives us direction and purpose. We can create freely, but our purpose is to serve man and creation with it. We may choose to end our days as God did his days of creation—by sitting down, reflecting, and considering it a good day. Our first priority is to do good and work in a manner that serves man and creation. In this way, we honor God, working for his glory.

This image of God on earth is given in a more concrete example in the New Testament through the personhood of Jesus Christ. Our image and likeness of God is corrupted by sin but gets a new, living interpretation through Christ. He is our example. He is man as God intended man to be— seeking the face of God and free from sin's entanglements. That is why God wants to recreate us as man in the image of his Son, Jesus Christ.[13] By sending Jesus into this world, God invites us to become as man was intended to be from the beginning.

Our role is to respond to this offer by choosing to dedicate ourselves to God and Jesus. God's role is to shape the new man in us. God does this by giving us the Holy Spirit, the divine nature within us. Our next challenge is to give this divine nature the place it deserves to shape our lives.

The inner freedom to choose is a part of God's design of creation. Our choice determines who we are and who we become. Divine nature wants to recreate us into people full of love, joy, peace, and patience. People who are friendly, good, and gentle. People with faith and self-control.[14]

When we embrace our humanity as Jesus did, our focus should turn to salvation. Jesus is the only one who could save the world, but as human beings and entrepreneurs, we can actually contribute to the salvation of the world. In addition to working on environmentally sustainable businesses or fighting poverty, as envoys of Christ, we want people saved from evil, from themselves, from judgment, and from destruction. This goes beyond providing prosperity, business successes, and moments of happiness. It is about helping people become reconciled with God. As Paul says, "Therefore, we are ambassadors for Christ, God making his appeal through us. We implore you on behalf of Christ, be reconciled to God."[15]

Being reconciled with God means that God considers us a part of himself. We are being united with him, and as a result, we become part of his realm, glory, majesty, and kingdom. A spin-off of this new unity is that God's favor is upon us and that he will always be with us and in us. God is no longer opposed to us but is always for us. To live according to God's nature and out of connection with him is the source of a real and full life.

We as reconciled entrepreneurs are free to live and act because everything belongs to God and, therefore, to us as well. The only limitation is that we use it in a way that is driven by love for God, others, creation, and ourselves. In other words, we are called to bless the world. Blessing the world out of love with God's ideas, promises, and presence is a delightful thing to do. As entrepreneurs, we have the means and skills to do this.

Connected People

God is a God of relationships—a God of connection, nearness, and care. That is who he is. This is also his name, as he states, "I am and will be there with you. I Am."[16] Jesus's name is Immanuel, *God with us*. All of God's character traits and personality traits are relational. He knows our difficulties, temptations, and pain as human beings from his own experience. He can, therefore, sympathize with us and help us.[17] When Jesus left the earth, he promised a comforter, the Holy Spirit, who will be nearby.

As God's image-bearers, we are relational people. We who are entrepreneurs and leaders have been given responsibility. As entrepreneurs, each of us exists in relation to something or someone who holds him to responsibility. We are not individual people who only live for ourselves. We have a responsibility to lead and care for others to the best of our abilities.

However, connecting and living in loving and sincere relationships is difficult today and under pressure. I encounter many entrepreneurs who are no longer connected to others, to themselves, their emotions, their feelings, or their physical health and bodies. As a result of this some think and act only from their understanding, and some are stressed or burned out.

I also meet entrepreneurs who are so deeply immersed in their own world that they are no longer able to connect with their clients and employees. They no longer know who they are as individuals or what they feel. I know people who have not learned to develop real, sincere, loving, and long-lasting relationships. Connection and sincere sustainable loving relationships are no longer an obvious aspect of life, yet connection and relationships are one of the most important aspects of business life and leadership today.

How can we reconnect with one another? Living and working in connection with one another requires skills other than the spreadsheet management that seems to be so popular in some MBA courses. It requires the transformation of our inner life and our very humanity into the image and resemblance of Jesus Christ by the power of the Holy Spirit. The Holy Spirit is God's power and influence on our existence, ready to shape our inner selves. A rooted identity helps in this, along with developing Christian virtues, such as faith, hope, and love.

2. To rule is to serve.

The second vocation is ruling by serving. Because in our society, the verb "to rule" is often loaded with connotations of the abuse of power, we must realize that in the Bible, the word implicates responsibility[18] and service.[19]

We are God's stewards on this earth. We read that man was created "…so that they may rule over the fish in the sea and the birds in the sky, over the livestock and all the wild animals, and over all the creatures that move along the ground."[20]

We are called to take care of and serve. In addition, Genesis 2:15 states, "The Lord God took the man and put him in the Garden of Eden to work it and take care of it."[21] We come across the words "work" and "take care." The word used here for work, means "work" but also "serve, honor, worship." With our work, we worship, honor, and serve God. Work is an act of worship.

The verb "to take care" also means "to protect." We come across these words often in the Old Testament when God's work for his people is described. And just as God protects his people, humanity must protect God's creation. We as witnesses and image-bearers are called to adopt a serving attitude in our work so that God is honored and his creation is treated as something to take care of and not to exploit. Jerusalem is characterized by its indifference to status and position and its focus on serving others. Jesus relinquished his greatness and equality with God to become human, choosing to serve.[22] As Christian Jerusalem entrepreneurs and image-bearers, we, too, are called to bless and serve with this attitude in mind.[23] During the last supper, Jesus said, "The kings of the Gentiles exercise lordship over them, and those in authority over them are called benefactors. But not so with you. Rather, let the greatest among you become as the youngest, and the leader as one who serves."[24]

In the Gospel of John, we read that during this last supper, when these words were spoken, Jesus added action to his words and washed his disciples' feet.[25] God humbled himself as a human being to wash other people's feet. In fact, God suffered and died to give others life and take their punishment. This is an unprecedented example of serving born out of love.

As an entrepreneur, we serve our clients not only for the goal of money but because we are interested in their well-being. As leaders within our company, we don't use our staff for our own benefit only, but we try to make them the people God intended them to be, working in their God-given talents with joy. Moreover, the company is called to become a serving force for the welfare of society. As a good friend told me, "All my companies need to be a force for good."

3. Be fruitful and multiply.

The third vocation is that of increasing or multiplying. In Genesis, this vocation is translated to procreation and having children to populate the earth.[26] The book of Genesis speaks of biological offspring. With Abraham, the offspring has another dimension and includes spiritual offspring.[27] Spiritual offspring isn't centered around a biological line but a spiritual and moral line.

When the Jews were arguing that they are the biological children of Abraham, Jesus said, "If you were Abraham's children, you would be doing the works Abraham did."[28] Jesus was actually saying that the Jews are not truly children of Abraham even though they are his biological offspring. His point was that children are those who act in accordance with what their father did. Jesus calls people who love him children of God because they love God. "If God were your father, you would love me, for God is the source of my being, and from him I come."[29] Paul sees all believers as children of Abraham.[30] He says, "...just as Abraham 'believed God, and it was counted to him as righteousness'? Know then that it is those of faith who are the sons of Abraham."[31] John calls God the Father of love and calls people who love children of God.[32]

As parents, we want to give our children the right values and standards. In the Old Testament, we are explicitly called upon to pass on the faith and God's words of life to the next generations.[33] As entrepreneurs and leaders, we have unique opportunities to put feet to this, enabling us to leave a spiritual legacy for those who come after.

Paul also sees forming spiritual children—and in this way becoming fruitful and multiplying—as investing in a new generation of leaders. Paul formulates this principle in this way: "...what you have heard from me in the presence of many witnesses entrust to faithful men, who will be able to teach others also." He sets out a strategy of multiplication. I encourage you to look for people who can pass on this precious gift of faith to others. Invest in these people and help them to become leaders of a new generation of leaders who can pass on the faith to their friends and to other new leaders.

I try to do this as well. My conviction is that the people I meet have been entrusted to me by God for a short or long period. Therefore, I want to give them the most valuable and worthy parts of my life. For me, this is the good news of Jesus and our future in God.

It is about the formation and not about selling the gospel.

Christ calls us to multiply by leaving spiritual children. He said, "Make disciples," people who want to be followers of Jesus and who want to live out the ideals of God and Jesus. Each of the Bible's four Gospels ends with a mission statement to pass on the gospel and make disciples of Christ.[34] This call is not about selling the gospel; it is not about convincing people of our truth; it is not about us solely talking about God and Jesus. Nor is it about winning souls. This vocation is about the spiritual offspring we leave behind. It is about the formation of children into mature people.

All people on this earth are works in progress. Many of them are looking to others to find the "right" way; therefore, we need to be a living letter they can read. Our life and behavior are part of God's revelation to man along with the Bible, creation, and God's speaking through His Spirit.

Jesus was God's living letter. He revealed God to his disciples by spending time with them and forming them throughout his ministry life. We can also share our time and our lives with others. For example, I know several entrepreneurs who consciously invest in a new generation by making themselves available as mentors, coaches, or spiritual fathers. Many Christian entrepreneurs share their lives with their business friends and pray for them. In this way, they want to show who God is.

This is something different than selling the gospel, which is exemplified by an entrepreneur called Bill. He once told me that, in addition to his visible turnover graphs, he kept a hidden scoreboard recording the number of "God talks" and the "decisions made" for God as a result of his talks. For him, this spiritual scoreboard was his entry pass into heaven, with the "jewels in his crown" dependent on his performance.

One day, a client confronted Bill with his behavior of selling Christ alongside his products, saying, "First you sell me a machine and ask for money. That's okay. But now you try selling me something vague called Christ and ask for my soul, the most precious thing I own. That's not okay. I'm canceling the order for the machine I just bought."

Bill spent time reflecting and praying. He realized his way of thinking and behaving was off, but he did not yet understand why. Then God spoke to him and said, "I'm not something that needs to be sold. Who do you think I am? I am God!" At that point, Bill began to understand that God was not for sale and that his role within the kingdom was not to be a salesperson. His role was limited to being a fellow human being.

When Bill now meets new people, he listens, asks questions, and sometimes he shares his personal experience. Everything Bill does is focused on a real and sincere encounter of the heart. He enjoys helping people find their way in life and discovering and getting to know God. Bill prays for people a lot and is sensitive to what they need. He is still willing to share something of his faith and his God whenever necessary, but now it happens out of love and when appropriate. When Bill realized he is no longer responsible for other people's choices, a burden was lifted, which gave him the authenticity, peace, and freedom he needed to have real encounters full of love and passion.

Sharing your faith and discipling people has nothing to do with a sales approach, a transaction, or a specific moment in our lives. Sharing your faith is equipping others to understand life from God's perspective. It is helping them to understand and trust God for life and the future. Faith is trusting God for who he is and that he is at work. This trust enables us to live in whatever life gives us, loving and living freely from that what is given to us as a gift. God's presence and his ability to merge our reality and brokenness for his goodness, glory, and majesty is the good news. The point is not what we do but what God does. He wants to change us more and more into his image and likeness. This renewal and transformation is our salvation.

God's Ambassador

> *My joy is in what God does and not what I do. The light in people's eyes and the smile on their faces when I tell them about the cross reminds me that God is allowing a spark to fly on dry wood, ready to be ignited. We have a message of love that can change the world because God is present in this love. Our faith is not about using the right techniques, but about God acting through us.*

This is a quote from Henry, a Christian Jerusalem entrepreneur who is aware that people look at him as a letter of God.[35] He understands that multiplication—having spiritual children walking in the ways of God—doesn't come by techniques but by the work of the Holy Spirit, who would like to work throughout him and us. He is an entrepreneur well-known for humbleness, although he is wealthy and has several factories in various nations. He dedicated his life to make Christ known as an entrepreneur in the marketplace. For him, these are not two worlds, but one.

Paul talks in this sense not only about readable letters but also about being an ambassador: "Therefore, we are ambassadors for Christ, God making his appeal through us. We implore you on behalf of Christ, be reconciled to God."[36] But despite this calling, many Christian entrepreneurs actually live their lives like tourists. They are excited and curious to explore and discover all life has to offer. They want to experience life in all its fullness without responsibility. Paul, however, isn't talking about tourism when writing about our identities and roles; he's talking about being an ambassador of Christ.

An ambassador represents a country or a king and speaks on his behalf. This means we as Christian Jerusalem entrepreneurs are Christ's representatives to the business world. We represent the realm of God and his kingdom. As ambassadors, we lead by initiating to others, inviting them to participate in the lives we have been given by God.

In this verse, Paul writes, "We are." Therefore, this is not a question or an option. As Christians, we represent Christ where we are. You hear people's opinions about God or Jesus by asking about their experiences with Christians. They may say things like, "If he is a Christian, then I don't want to have anything to do with this God." Our business choices, our business conduct, and what we say are of the utmost importance as ambassadors of Christ. Our challenges as ambassadors are not just about personal or business advantages but also about how our choices and behavior reflect God to others. Think of the well-known words of Francis of Assisi: "Preach the gospel at all times, and if necessary, use words."

Maybe some Christians are thinking, "If my behavior and actions influence someone's opinion about God, then I'd better not reveal my Christianity. After all, I'm not perfect. My behavior doesn't always reflect who Christ is." But it is exactly these people who should be more transparent and open. It's not about being or becoming perfect. We may strive for excellence within our abilities, but we don't need to achieve a certain level of perfection. The basis of the Christian faith lies in God's grace and not in our actions. By showing that we are the same as others, we make the gospel available to everyone. The gospel is not exclusively for "good" people; it is for everyone. The amazing thing is that God, despite who we are, loves us. We would fail if we only showed our good sides.

Helping people understand and love God is the best you can give to others; it is the best legacy you can leave behind. It benefits personal lives and impacts society.

What do we leave behind?

Now that we have discussed the idea of leaving a legacy by multiplication, we should also look at its spin-off in society. How does this calling of multiplication and leaving spiritual children influence future generations and impact lives? I once read a study about the legacy of two different people, Max Jukes and Jonathan Edwards.[37] The first one was a criminal and a murderer. The second was a preacher. Both men lived in the 18th century. The researchers examined the legacies and successors of both men over a period of 150 years. Here are their findings:

Max Jukes	**Jonathan Edwards**
7 murderers	300 preachers
60 thieves	295 experts in their field
67 lived with sexual disorders	100 missionaries
100 alcoholics	100 lawyers
200+ involved in prostitution	80 in the government
300 died before their time	1 vice president
	13 senators
	1 governor
	75 army officers
	65 professors

Two different people, two different legacies. As Christian entrepreneurs, we also want to leave something behind, but what? A successful company making a good profit or the DNA of a company on which business is built? A profitable company can quickly turn into a failing company, but if I leave behind the right DNA, personality, character, skills, and talents to build and run a profitable company, then I leave something bigger behind. Something that can grow, multiply, and leave a lasting legacy.

I have to think back to my good friend I mentioned earlier, who believes his companies and endeavors should be a force for good. He is now training and educating his children on how to keep these companies alive as a force for good. In this way, he is multiplying what was given to him for generations still to come.

4. Loving Others

The next calling or vocation we identify is loving others. Love should be the driving force of everything we do as entrepreneurs. The apostle Paul says that our actions don't count if they are not driven by love.[38] Our ambitions drive our thinking and actions. Our actions and behavior define our results and our destination. If love does not govern our being, ambitions, and mindset, something else will. That will then define our results and destination, ending up in Babylon.

Love needs to be the source that saturates everything we do because love is the attribute that makes life worth living; it is the only source that makes our service as entrepreneurs authentic and true. Love changes the way we see things and, therefore, it defines our decisions and the way we act in situations. Love makes society and relationships flourish.

We are connected to other people and the rest of creation. Our task is not only to care for them[39] but also to love them with divine *agape* love, as discussed and elaborated on in the previous chapter.[40] After all, we are God's image-bearers. Jesus expressed how we must do this when he said, "You shall love the Lord your God with all your heart and with all your soul and with all your mind. This is the great and first commandment. And a second is like it: You shall love your neighbor as yourself."[41]

In addition, in the Gospel of John and in the first letter of John, we find the call to love. This divine *agape* love, which functions as our source, gives us the power and motivation that can overcome any resistance and pain. Because of this characteristic, as Paul says, it can endure anything and perseveres in everything.[42] This love, which has become visible through Jesus' death on the cross, is a tremendous power, which eventually defeats everything and conquers all other forces.[43] This love is also a verb, something that can work in us. For the practical implementation of this love in our companies and business operations, see the chapter "Love in Business."

5. Serving in a Specific Place or Role

You serve at your specific place and within your current role or job. Serving from a special place or specific role often has to do with our daily work and role in society. For example, we have roles as fathers or mothers, managers, and entrepreneurs. With our role comes responsibility.

We are not set in place by accident if we believe that God is involved in all we do. Our specific personalities, our personal life experience, our unique talents, our beliefs, and our circumstances all contribute to a unique way of fulfilling this task. We have the freedom to uniquely shape this position. Every person has his own path and part to play;[44] a unique role is given to each of us by God. In searching for our unique role, we should not compare ourselves to others or just seek to have it all;[45] rather, we should make use of the position, talents, and possibilities that have been uniquely given to us.

In a free society with countless opportunities, we can look for the job or role that fits our personality and gifting. It is rather unique in the context of human history that so many of us can choose this ourselves. It is wonderful to be able to express our personal and unique talents within our jobs, making both life and work much more enjoyable. There are training opportunities and courses designed to help you discover your unique qualities and determine your unique place in (working) life.[46] This goal or job is often an extension of how you are designed and made, which values you find important, and your life experience.

Maybe you don't have the luxury of doing the work you love right now because circumstances have forced you into different work—you had to take over the business from your parents, or there is unemployment in your nation and you just have to make a living. In one of these scenarios, it is important to use your spare time to do something meaningful for you. If the work you do sometimes limits the enjoyment of your unique talents, volunteering and hobbies can become important for your personal development and expression. Despite the limited time, this can be very freeing and rewarding. In this case, your work is a source of income to make something else possible. The calling within your work remains, however. You are still called within your work to be a loving person with a focus on loving relationships, serving others, being fruitful, and being an image-bearer of God and Christ out of our unity with Christ.

Your Calling as an Entrepreneur

As we said at the start of this chapter, your calling defines your *why* and forms your *what* and *how*. How is calling working in your specific role as an entrepreneur? Jerusalem entrepreneurs make a clear distinction between *what* they do and *why* they do it. When asked *why* they do their work or *why* they run their business a certain way, they answer with something like, "To make God and his Kingdom visible in this world." If you ask *what* they do, the answer may be, "I build houses or I produce screw compressors," depending on their profession. *What* they do is an extension of their passions, personality, and qualities. *Why* they do it is related to their calling. Let me give you two examples to explain this further.

Eric was an entrepreneur in an emerging niche in the food industry. His business was booming and profitable, with many investors who wanted to buy his company. He could get an incredible amount of money for his business if he sold it. When asked why he didn't sell, he answered, "God has made me a good entrepreneur, and I see this as my calling and responsibility to God. I want to serve and honor God, people, and society with my business skills."

Eric knew that he was equipped as an entrepreneur and that he was good in his role of being an entrepreneur. He also knew that the day he sold his business, he would deny his calling as an entrepreneur for God. He didn't work for himself, but for God. He didn't work to become rich, but to serve people and society with his expertise and services.

I also have to think of Alexander, a smart businessman. His vision and perceived calling are to create jobs and help the region he lives in grow and prosper economically. Alexander has many businesses, and he makes a lot of money these days, but he doesn't care much about this because that's not his motivation. That is not *why* he is doing what he does. His calling is to create jobs in his region and make it prosper.

Money and business success are merely tools. He experiences a lot of contentment and fulfillment in his entrepreneurship and endeavors because he is creating jobs, serving people, and making God known, but not for the money. Sincere and successful Christian entrepreneurs know the limited value of money for personal happiness, but they also know the power of money as a tool to create new business for God and bless others with work and opportunities.

6. Living in Unity

We can understand our vocations and even walk in them, but whether we also bear fruit in our calling is a separate matter. Connecting with Christ in our daily lives is crucial. If we dwell in Christ and Christ dwells in us, we can ask whatever we want and we will bear fruit as his disciples.[47] This indwelling determines true success and real fruit. True success as a Christian Jerusalem entrepreneur is not about making a profit or increasing your market share as an entrepreneur but being a true disciple of Christ.[48] In this way, Christ can work through our business as we are open to serve him with our business. The love of Christ that flows through our actions is to the glory of God and may stir up the desire in humanity to find the love that is in Christ.

Every Christian Jerusalem entrepreneur shapes this connection and indwelling in his own way. I know a businesswoman named Mary who sees her car as her private cathedral. She sings, listens, keeps silent, and meditates to listen for God's voice in traffic jams. In this way, she relates to God on a daily basis; she experiences God's love and works out of this love in her daily business life. It is amazing to see how other people value her attitude and way of doing business. Many conversations are sparked by the way she operates; often, her behavior awakens a desire in others to know more about the secret of her loving relationship with Christ.

I know of entrepreneurs who regularly celebrate the Eucharist (communion) to express their unity with Christ and receive God's grace. Others have a special room or chair in their homes to reflect on life, pray, and read the Bible. Others like to walk in nature. All of these entrepreneurs have in common their desire to share their life with Christ and be with him. At these moments, God has the opportunity to speak into being-growth in their lives.

This unity is not only very effective in being a true disciple filled with God's love and Spirit but is also God's desire.[49] It is for this reason that God created us, that Jesus died for us, and that the Holy Spirit would like to dwell within us. This unity with God is the centrality of the good news of the gospel. God wants to share his life, glory, majesty, and kingdom with us human beings. For us as entrepreneurs, this unity with God is a reward in itself; it gives us joy, but it is also shaping our actions into a force for good. We live out of this relationship and are inspired by it. What an amazing message.

5

Living in Connection

Living in connection is the second on our list of essential characteristics of a Christian Jerusalem entrepreneur.[1] We can distinguish three types of connection:

- Being connected with God, the source of all blessings and love. This shapes the direction in which we are moving.
- Being connected with ourselves and being whole. This implies striving to be one and whole in every aspect of our being. God desires that we become the person he intended. This makes us more human and positively shapes our credibility, trustworthiness, and integrity. These last aspects are of huge importance in business. The currency in business is not money, but trust.
- Being connected to others. This connection needs to be driven by love; otherwise, we will use others and act like the prostitute of Babylon. Instead of using others, the Christian Jerusalem entrepreneur wants others to flourish.

Being Whole and Connected to God

The most important connection for us as Christian Jerusalem entrepreneurs is the connection with God and our whole self. Out of this we can connect with others and develop a healthy life that is blessing others.

I meet many people who lead a double life. They are Christians in name but don't live up to it. They are not inwardly connected and one. This is a huge problem. The important thing is that in all respects, we are solid and whole; all parts of our humanity are connected and speak the same message. We must be non-fragmented people, true and reliable, with whom feeling, thinking, doing, and being coincide—people who do not abuse the name of God for personal gain or justification.

As Christians, we want to live in complete unity with God and Jesus. Although we have two natures in us, a broken and sinful nature and a new divine nature, the challenge is to dwell in God in such a way that he controls our feeling, thinking, being, and doing.

In the Sermon on the Mount, Jesus talks about the righteousness of the Pharisees (the spiritual elite of the time).[2] The Pharisees were focused on rules and deeds without anchoring God's values and words of life in their hearts. They were fragmented. "Doing" was separated from their hearts, their feelings, and their desires. Jesus says that following the rules alone is not enough, that God's righteousness goes deeper than following commandments. Becoming righteous involves a heart transformation with consequences in what we do. Jesus says:

> You have heard that it was said to those of old, "You shall not murder; and whoever murders will be liable to judgment." But I say to you that everyone who is angry with his brother will be liable to judgment.[3]

> You have heard that it was said, "You shall not commit adultery." But I say to you that everyone who looks at a woman with lustful intent has already committed adultery with her in his heart.[4]

These are challenging words of Jesus. He cares about humanity's wholeness and unity with God because God is the source of love; without being connected to him, we lose ourselves as God's people, disciples, and stewards. If we separate parts of our lives from God, for example, our business life or our family life, we live a dual life and others will intuitively feel that. This may mean that we will eventually lose our credibility as Christians. Righteousness is not about what we do but about who we are. We need to embrace God's words and values as the sole longing we have for life, as the ideal and desire we want to live up to. We want to "become" like Jesus and not just "do" as Jesus did.

At the end of his teaching about the righteousness of the Pharisees, Jesus says that we must start to look like God. "Be perfect, as your Heavenly Father is perfect."[5] Perfection here is not a moral issue of undivided goodness but a process in which we grow to become more fully the people of God, which we are called to as image-bearers of Christ. It is about maturity, fullness, and perfection in goodness and being—wholly undivided in every respect and completely merged with the divine nature of our God, Lord, and Savior. This will be our future, which Christ has died for and, by his death and resurrection, made us new beings. This reality can also be lived today, although still in brokenness.

Connecting with Everything You Are

Another way of experiencing unity and being connected to our whole self is the connection between our rational mind, feelings and emotions, spiritual life, and physical body. All four need to be interconnected in order to be fully human. We are much more than our rational minds. Human beings have emotions and feelings, and as soon as we close ourselves off from them, some of our humanity dies. Sometimes we discover a hardness that we didn't think was possible.

I know of an entrepreneur who bought another company. He discovered that one of the older and lesser-skilled employees in this company used very expensive company equipment to serve some of his personal friends in private. This was an opportunity to dismiss this employee, which would lower the operational costs. Because he was not connected to his emotions and feelings, it was a merely rational decision to him. He felt no compassion. His decision destroyed the future and life of a faithful employee who worked in this company for more than 40 years just three years before retirement. Later, when he got more in touch with his personal feelings, he regretted this and even considered it an unethical, unnecessary decision.

In these moments of inner-disconnection, where we are not connected with our emotions and feelings, we can use and exploit people or justify child labor with an appeal to competition and market forces. It's in those moments of hardness that we easily ignore our feelings and justify our behavior by saying, "This is not my responsibility" or "I didn't know or recognize what was going on."

Being Connected to Others

Loving relationships and living in connection with others are societal game changers. If we can live from a deep sense of connectedness and love, everything changes. It makes a difference if we see someone as a fellow human being we love, know, and are related to rather than an object to use, a competitor, or costs on the profit and loss statement, as in the Babylon thinking. It makes a difference to meet someone and look them in the eye rather than talking about someone in the abstract, without relationship.

If we're able to make contact with someone, a lot can change. These sincere encounters make space for compassion and friendship.

Take Bert, who had an aversion to foreigners, refugees, and migrants. He thought it would be better if they left the country. And then he found himself in a refugee camp on a trip in Jordan and came into contact with the "Other." Other is purposefully written with a capital O, as Levinas, a French philosopher, does to express its uniqueness and specialness. This experience changed Bert's opinion and erased his prejudices.

The Threat to Real Connection

Creating a connection is perhaps one of the greatest challenges of our current time. Individualism in Western societies is at its height, and polarization is on the rise; we talk more and more in terms of "us and them." We live fragmented lives in bubbles. We look for like-minded people from the same social class.

We see this in business as well. Many business leaders feel lonely. They feel that they are even alone at work or in a crowd of people. This sense of loneliness exists even in supposedly intimate relationships like marriages, friendships, or between parents and children. Even in intimate sexual encounters, people can feel completely lonely and lost. Being dependent on another is perceived as scary because it feels like losing control. For them, being fully known and loved without conditions or restraint is unthinkable. For many, real love and being known are scary; they aren't aware of the importance of vulnerability in a healthy, sustainable relationship. For some, to be known and loved anyway is no longer a goal. It's either too difficult or too good to be true. Fear drives away the possibility of being known and loved.

I once had a brainstorming session with business people from different generations on the theme of meeting and connecting. The older generation preferred personal meetings, while the younger generation relied more on online meetings. This was a recognizable difference. One woman told me, for example, that she preferred connecting online because it made it easier for her to walk away from a conversation. If she didn't like it, she could leave the conversation without feeling guilty. She wanted to be in control and be able to decide for herself whether conversations could become personal or could be kept at a distance.

Another young business person said, "I share different areas of my life with different people. That's why personal encounters are difficult, because I never know what they'll ask me. Online, I can control everything and just send them the answers I like to give." What struck me, however, was the next sentence: "Imagine if they knew me completely; what would they think of me? Would they still love me if they knew me completely? I don't think so. Therefore, I share certain parts of my life with certain people and don't give anyone the full picture. This is easier to do online. Therefore, I try to avoid personal meetings in real life."

We also see this fear for real encounters at network meetings. We see many people who are more concerned about themselves and their compulsion to present a good profile than about connecting. Their fear of rejection determines the way they enter a meeting. They control and direct the conversation with questions, humorous remarks, and brilliant comments without showing vulnerability. The goal is not to have a real encounter where they can get to know each other but to display themselves as they want to be seen. Real relationships die this way because there is no real person to connect

Next to this we also see many entrepreneurs and business leaders living in a bubble, no longer connected to the real lives of others or even their own realities. Out of these disconnected lives, great scandals, born of arrogance, have arisen, offering evidence of this disconnect from reality—scandals where business leaders feel like they are above the law or even are the law. They have made decisions that go outside the legal framework. Think, for example, of the private use of business funds and resources, side letters in deals and transactions, the use of double books, and a special department used to reach personal ambitions and goals of the president without being supervised by the board of directors or the legal department of the company.

Overcoming Fear

Fear is one of the greatest driving forces. Many people feel anxious and insecure without control in their lives, while still others feel like victims of their circumstances. A victim mentality seems to be a dominant theme in our time.[6] A key characteristic of the victim mentality is that *someone else* is to blame for my discomfort. We can solve our discomfort if we remove the "Other" from our lives.

Ultimately, a culture of fear and a predominant victim mentality leads to authoritarian power and power abuse. Populist and autocratic business leaders position themselves as the solution. They desire to control and protect themselves from others. This is not a path we should want to take as Jerusalem entrepreneurs. Love, however, drives out fear.[7]

When I love someone, I am not afraid of him; I want to get to know him, and I feel responsibility and compassion. With love, our differences are no longer threatening; instead, we discuss our differences so we get to know and appreciate each other. Love is the key to real encounters and real connections. Love shapes healthy and sustainable relationships in companies and in societies. All true connection is founded on love.

6

Love as the Foundation

Jesus promised that love is the basis for a full and abundant life. Love should be the primary driver of a Christian Jerusalem entrepreneur. Every other driver moves away from God, his kingdom, and a full and abundant life for everyone. We do business to honor God and create a life by serving the stakeholders and ourselves.

Love is the core characteristic of God. It was because of love that God reached out to humanity through Christ. "For God so loved the world, that he gave his only Son, that whoever believes in him should not perish but have eternal life."[1] Love as a business concept is discussed in the chapter "Love in Business." In our current chapter, we focus on love in a different way—namely, as a characteristic of "being" and as the foundation of connection.

Without love as a driver for connection and relationships, we will start to use others for our own benefit like the prostitute of Babylon is doing. Without love, we will primarily work for results. Business is a tool to love others and a tool to express our love for others. Without love, a business will lose its original purpose to serve people and bless society with our endeavors. Losing this love creates the Babylonian society and marketplace we find ourselves in nowadays. Love has to flow out of our inner being, as Christ is making us a person of love.

God is the source of love.

What we mean by *love* is formed throughout our upbringing and based on our personal experiences. Therefore, it could be that the understanding of love is polluted by bad experiences. For a good understanding of love, we need the original source of love: God.

God is the original source of love and of all existence.[2] He wants to make us a source of love.[3] We are people wanted by God; otherwise, we wouldn't exist. That is why God loves us unconditionally—he created us to be loved by him and to share his life and majesty with us. Brokenness in our lives does not equate a barrier to this unconditional love. He loves us as we are and wants to be present in our brokenness. He wants to comfort people and help them to accept themselves. God wants to teach people to love themselves and others as he loves us. Living this kind of love isn't easy, as we all know from experience. Too often, we have too little love, we express our love in the wrong way, or our love is rejected. Loving hurts and often includes disappointment and rejection. That's why it's important to intentionally choose to love. Every act of love has meaning for those who receive it; this love needs to be embraced and celebrated. Love is the irreplaceable center of an abundant life.

Self-love is a condition to love others.

In the Bible, we are called upon to love the Other with the same love we have for ourselves. Jesus summarizes God's intention and commandments as follows, "You shall love the Lord your God with all your heart and with all your soul and with all your mind. This is the great and first commandment. And a second is like it: You shall love your neighbor as yourself."[4] Meeting, connecting, and loving begins with the way we connect to our true selves. This determines all the other relationships and connections we have. The questions we need to ask ourselves are these:

Do I love myself? Do I accept and love who I am? A healthy love of self is a prerequisite for loving others well.

If I love myself too little, I cannot love others properly because love is, among other things, giving yourself to the other person. But what can I give of myself if I don't love myself? When I do not love myself, I want to hide, becoming unavailable to others. Love also means allowing myself to be seen so the other person can love me. If I'm hiding, what is he or she loving? The image I've carefully created and the carefully constructed life that I've deemed acceptable? This is not me; it's what I'm pretending to be. In the end, I remain empty and lonely in this love. How can I overcome my loneliness if I am not fully known and accepted? How can anyone know me if I don't reveal who I really am?

Self-esteem and loving oneself are also important qualities in drawing boundaries, especially in our work lives. If I don't find myself valuable, why should someone else? If I continuously dismiss myself, where do others draw the line? Self-esteem gives me an identity, communicating that I am too valuable to be abused, whether it be by an employee, manager, or colleague.

Only when I have sufficient self-esteem and when I can love myself properly can I love without expecting anything in return. Giving and receiving are part of the beautiful dance of love; giving with the expectation of receiving is not. The latter is a transaction or manipulation. When my self-love is healthy, I also want to receive because I know I am worthy of love. Without a healthy love of self, I keep giving just to get attention called love or hoping to receive what I need.

Destructive Forms of Self-Love

If I only give to receive, I quickly come to forms of self-love that characterize many entrepreneurs: narcissism, selfishness, and egocentrism. These are destructive traits because they do not take others into account and ultimately drive those who are suffering from them into loneliness and many types of unhealthy behaviors. The urge to prove oneself is often stronger than healthy, beneficial virtues or ethics.

Narcissism is a behavior characterized by an obsession with oneself. This form of self-love is often accompanied by selfishness, dominance, an exaggerated form of ambition, an unhealthy focus on status symbols, and a lack of empathy.

Selfishness, also known as egoism, is a human trait in which one strives for one's successes and happiness while neglecting the interests and well-being of others. A healthier form of egoism is when we find fulfillment and purpose in the well-being of the people we live with or in the joy of the community of which we are apart. We say, "If the people around me are joyful and happy, I am, too." The negative form of egoism doesn't care about the well-being of others. His motto is, "If I'm successful and happy, everyone around me must be happy."

Egocentrism is a diminished ability to put oneself in the shoes of another person. The result is that the person focuses on his own vision and interests and often assumes that his focus and priorities must be the focus and priorities of everyone else.

Many entrepreneurs are driven by one of these three negative forms of self-love. A good example is Tom. On the outside, Tom appeared to be a successful entrepreneur in real estate. This was not so much because of his own performance but because he inherited the company from his dad. If you heard him talk, you would think that all he owned came from his own efforts and business instinct. He loved himself in an unhealthy way and desired to be a successful real estate trader. In public, he failed to tell that he inherited the company and that it was successful because of the abilities of an excellent team of dedicated and zealous workers. Many started to worship Tom for his success and the way he spoke. Many times, Tom bullied his qualified staff and fired people who spoke against him. He didn't allow people to do this because it would harm his dominant leadership and success stories.

Over time, Tom ended up with lousy people around him who were just there to profit from his wealth. They enjoyed the parties he threw and were willing to satisfy his need for self-affirmation. Soon after that, the company started to lose money. Year after year, it went from bad to worse. Tom felt more and more lonely and his need for affirmation became even stronger, forcing him to go after tangible, short-term successes that harmed the long-term goals and lasting health of the company.

The day then came when creditors came to talk about repaying the debts. He started to accuse them and fight them because he couldn't see the reality he himself had created. His whole world of success and self-confirmation started to burst. But despite this, he didn't change his lifestyle and behavior. Although the end would come irrevocably, just like the end of Babylon, he couldn't face it because he was blinded by his pride and unhealthy self-love.

Many entrepreneurs are driven and blinded by one of these three negative forms of self-love. The culture in the company is all about glorifying them as a leader, and most times, they go into self-destructive behavior to keep this dream going and to gain the adoration of the shareholders of the company. Some start to have a second, secret bookkeeping system; others produce side letters when they buy companies to make a huge profit later. Still others close the research and development department to lower the costs so that they have a better rating at the stock exchange, but with this, they destroy the company's future. God, through the Holy Spirit, wants to transform these forms of destructive self-love into healthy self-love that includes God and our fellow human beings.

Healthy Self-Love

A healthy love of self is given to us by others and protected by boundaries. If all is well, we were raised with unconditional love.

It was given to us by parents, friends, neighbors, etc. This love has made us who we are.

God is the source of true unconditional love. As John says, "We love because he first loved us."[5] This love of God is given to us by Christ, and it is up to us as human beings to receive and accept this love. A relationship comes about by receiving this love; a new unity is forged between God and man.

If we have come to know and accept this love for ourselves, then we are free to love others.

Rejection hurts and is not pleasant, but healthy love can look at the other who is expressing anger or disapproval with compassion. A healthy love sees that the other person is unable to love properly because of his own wounds or upbringing.

God's love for me allows me to love myself wherever I am without shame or self-condemnation. After all, it is because of this love that Christ came to earth to reconcile us with God. He made this love visible, tangible, and available to us. Today, we can experience this love when the Holy Spirit is in us. The Holy Spirit would like to heal us in such a way that we can receive, accept, and experience this love. Christ opened the door for him.

I realize these are big words. Too often we fail in experiencing and living out this divine love. But every day that I can catch a glimpse of it or share this love is an unspeakable joy and a day worth living.

7

Performance Drive

I'd like to tell you about an entrepreneur, Hubert, who grew up in a poor family. He heard his parents arguing about the cost of his education, worried about making ends meet. He became bitter about his life and his parents' financial situation. One night, after yet another fight at home, he told himself, *I will never be poor.*

Hubert became successful and rich, but he was also a hard businessman. With his fighter mentality, he conquered every setback. Strength, discipline, and perseverance were his keys to success. He used people and saw them as either instruments or competitors. Hubert had become what he wanted to be: rich. "Rich" had also become his identity. *I am a rich and successful entrepreneur. I don't need anything.* These words should sound familiar. That's right, Hubert had bought into the Babylonian mentality, and his fierce commitment to avoid poverty was what drove him.

Despite his wealth, Hubert's deep pain from the past had not disappeared. That pain helped him to go beyond the natural borders of his physical well-being, beyond normal ethics, to places others avoid. Hubert could work endlessly, completely focused on achieving his business ambitions. Sometimes he became irrationally angry, which made people afraid of him. This mostly happened when something didn't work out or when he didn't get his way. Hubert could also become incredibly dominant if he was afraid of losing control. Rules no longer applied to Hubert; he *was* the law.

Because of his financial success and his subsequent behavior, Hubert lost contact with the real world. He felt lonely. Only true, unconditional love could save him, yet he kept holding people at arm's length. People couldn't get close. Hubert didn't want to be loved; Hubert wanted to conquer and be appreciated. He wanted control over his own life, stemming from his fear of being poor like his parents. In the end, this Babylonian thinking dominated Hubert's life, causing him to be poor in relationships and love.

Performance drive can interfere with healthy connections, love, and real encounters, which are part of our second characteristic for the Christian Jerusalem-entrepreneur. We are called to connect.

Many entrepreneurs wouldn't claim to be driven by love. They act based on experiences and losses from the past, wanting to overcome them by proving themselves. Think of the unconscious desire to be seen and approved by a father or mother, especially by those whose parents have rejected them. Think of compensating for painful experiences from the past, such as being bullied in school or growing up in poverty.

The normal desire to prove yourself, to be recognized and seen, can become negative if it originates from an experience of loss. The actions and motivations of these entrepreneurs soon coincide with their carefully built identity, in which they find their drive. They want to overcome and compensate for the pain they experienced in the past. Their identity becomes characterized by statements like *I am better, I am different, I can cope with this world. See what I did? I am great!* They are continuously seeking respect, appreciation, and acceptance.

Pain as a Primary Driver

In Hubert's story, we see the power of personal drive. Our ambitions born out of upbringing and experiences drive us and determine the direction in which we go. A strong inner drive to push the boundaries, become successful, and make an outstanding performance is often a call for recognition and attention. This drive often results in the types of performances many shareholders and owners are looking for in their managers. They use these people to grow business and maximize profits. Often, shareholders and owners (as well as society) see these kinds of people as heroes, but in fact, they are the people for whom we should feel pity. As leaders, we can take advantage of someone's past pain. We can look for managers and staff who are wounded and hurt. Hurting people need to be cared for and not misused to our advantage. Sadly, the aforementioned scenarios all too often occur within our current business culture. Instead of offering ways to heal, we offer status, money, and the attention that will keep them going for the sake of business growth.

These types of managers and owners, who are hurt by their past and work limitlessly to prove themselves, are also very dangerous for the company because they are willing to play with high stakes that most businesses can't handle. They dare to cross the borders of the law if that benefits personal success. For example, some cheat with facts and figures.

Think of shifting the numbers of quarterly turn-over or complicating the company's financial model in such a way that accountants can be misled so that the company appears to be in better shape than it is. There have been many scandals caused by these types of leaders—who are no longer connected to reality, who live only for themselves, and who live by their own rules. Because of their special achievements, they are lauded and admired and feel like gods in their own worlds. Power, manipulation, and bending the rules slowly become commonplace.

A well-known motto within the Babylonian business culture is *It's only a crime if you get caught.* This often works well for a time, but when things go wrong, and things often go wrong, the whole company goes under with its leader. In high positions with responsibility, the need to compensate for failure with high performance is a dangerous combination. As owners and responsible leaders, and as Jerusalem entrepreneurs, we should avoid this trap and set ourselves apart by being aware of where our drives originate.

Embrace your past.

To be a successful Jerusalem entrepreneur, we must embrace all of ourselves, including our past experiences. We need to see all of it as something that belongs to us. The way to recovery is through having a safe place where you can be yourself without judgment—a kind of home, a place where you are fully known and fully loved. Only when we know this place can we learn to accept ourselves.

God wants to provide such an unconditionally safe place—a place without judgment and rejection, full of love and grace. From there, we can grow toward forgiveness for what has been done to us or taken away from us. From the inner peace and recovery that forgiveness brings, new love can grow. This love then becomes a force in our existence and a healthy drive in our work. From this love, we can serve and enter equal and healthy relationships with those who have been entrusted to us in the workplace.

Feedback is a gift.

It is crucial to surround yourself with a team of advisors, with people who are given permission to contradict you if needed. A pitfall for a healthy and sustainable business is to surround yourself with people who have similar personalities or who think along the same lines as you. In that case, you will only receive self-affirmation, which feels good but is not healthy for you or for the company. I remember talking to Eddie, who confided in me that whenever he saw the company controller entering his room, he got upset because this controller would probably have a message to correct him. The controller seldom came with good news. Most times, he would come in unexpectedly to point out some potential risks of decisions already made.

He complained to me, "This controller never considers the potential business opportunities I have in mind when I make decisions; he is only coming to point out the risk. This is so depressing.'" I asked him why he kept this guy in such an important position, even as part of the management team, if he felt this way about him. Then Eddie told me, "But without him, I will be lost. He already prevented me from making many mistakes. I just hate it when he speaks against me, but I know that he prevents me from making bad decisions. He is probably the best person who could come to me. I need him to protect me against myself and my ambition." Eddie is a wise entrepreneur who understands the value of feedback. His business is flourishing.

Also, our life partners often speak the truth in our lives. This can sometimes be difficult and irritating, but it is valuable. After all, they know us best. Having good and close friendships is also important. I mean the kind of friends who dare to speak the truth and with whom we can share even our secret lives.

Participating in accountability groups is also a good tool to stay on the right track. In most countries, Christian organizations foster these kinds of meetings.[1] We need others to maintain a good and healthy course. Look for a variety of personalities and backgrounds—ones different than your own. Find people with life experience and wisdom, not people who are still in the process of proving themselves.

8

Entrepreneurial Qualities

I'd like to tell you about my good friend James, who is an example of a great entrepreneur. He owns a leading company in logistics in his nation. What I value most in him is his humbleness, although he is very successful. He never boasts about himself; he always puts others first. When there is a time of crisis, he is on the floor with his employees, talking with them and encouraging them. He is also one of my mentors because of his insights and wisdom. He works and lives for a purpose bigger than himself and wants to see his companies be forces for good. I consider his personality, character, and talents to be the basis of his success. James has a combination of remarkable entrepreneurial qualities.

God-given entrepreneurial qualities are the third characteristic of a Christian Jerusalem entrepreneur. The Christian Jerusalem entrepreneur senses he has been given certain qualities from God to do business, and he takes this responsibility seriously. What are the essential qualities of a good entrepreneur, making it possible for him to take risks to realize his dreams? Throughout my life, I recognize that those who have the qualities to be entrepreneurs can be described as follows:

- *Trustworthy*. Trust is the currency of doing business. A trustworthy person is one with integrity. People must be able to trust you and build from there. Only then can good collaborations develop fruitful businesses. Clients, suppliers, shareholders, and employees are looking for reliable partners. Integrity gives you a head start in the market, while also contributing to effectiveness and efficiency since distrust, lawsuits, and other legal situations won't play a part in the thinking and conducting of the business.
- *Visionary*. Those who live and work with the end in mind can see dreams and goals realized according to Stephen Covey.[1] We are not determined by our past, but by our future.
- *Persevering and driven*. Answering the question of *why* we do things drives us. It's not only important to know the motivation but to use it in a good way, which gives us meaning, energy, and helps us to develop perseverance. These qualities are essential in overcoming resistance and reaching the goal. Discipline supports, but in itself, it is not a motivational power.
- *Wise*. Wisdom is the experience and the ability to judge and understand circumstances and people, as well as the market. It helps you read the times and work on timing and the right partnerships, all of which are crucial for success. Wisdom also helps us stay grounded and prioritize well. It helps us realize our goals in a practical and economically profitable way.

- *Curious and inquisitive.* A good entrepreneur has a curious and inquisitive mindset. He observes well, reads widely, and wants to uncover the essence of things to understand them. This curiosity helps him add new products and services to society from his wider understanding.
- *Courageous.* A good entrepreneur is brave. Despite the difficulties and uncertainties that he acknowledges, he dares to explore paths others do not naturally choose. This also inspires others to be courageous, ignore existing conventions, and explore the world and its possibilities freely.
- *Good communicator.* Open, respectful, and consistent communication wins the minds and hearts of all stakeholders. Communicating well serves to both inspire them and win their favor for your ideas. Think about the decisions you have to make and how you need the favor of your investors, banks, shareholders, and employees to support this decision; otherwise, you cannot execute your plans well.
- *Humorous and well-mannered.* Both qualities are keys to good and lasting relationships in the workplace. Whether it's clients, business partners, CEOs, or employees, these qualities help to create a good atmosphere, help people with varying perspectives and worldviews work with one another, and remind someone that he is valued and esteemed. Humor is helpful to overcome difficulties and quarrels.
- *Loyal.* Good entrepreneurs can be inspirational in how they remain loyal to themselves and their goals. They protect their purpose and stay

grounded. They are people with both a backbone and a goal in mind.

- *Hands-on.* These entrepreneurs aren't stuck in discussing theories; they are also putting them into action. An entrepreneur creates things, and his dreams and convictions are expressed in this work and creativity.

Of course, specific talents—such as financial and legal knowledge—can contribute in a positive way to the progress of the entrepreneur but are not especially necessary for entrepreneurship to flourish since it can be outsourced.

Unrecognized Qualities

Arthur is a young, successful entrepreneur. I met him on a business trip. He has a huge business with subsidiaries in various nations, and he has a great personality. Arthur's drive is to honor and serve God with his company. In my encounters with him, I discovered that Arthur was not highly educated, but he is curious, perceptive, and has the practical understanding to observe and understand things. He values people and knows how to achieve what he wants to achieve. Arthur has street smarts gained from his childhood experiences.

He talked about his impoverished childhood and how hungry he was. He told me about the violence and alcoholism that surrounded him as a little boy. An elderly woman took care of him and fed him as she was able. She taught Arthur love and introduced him to Jesus Christ. This combination of being able to survive on the streets and the new values of love and service made him a great entrepreneur. He had never heard of an MBA (Master of Business Administration), but I advised Arthur to pursue it. Ultimately, he was not admitted to the university because he didn't have a diploma. According to their criteria, he was too unskilled.

Arthur has a multi-million-dollar company, but this educational system did not think he was good enough to enroll in their university. Our society has become much too focused on knowledge and not on wisdom and other hidden qualities. A wise person can prioritize what kind of knowledge and information is important and what is not. He is also able to utilize knowledge by applying it to practical daily reality. Moreover, a wise person can see a greater perspective in the midst of various facts and figures.

I speak to many successful entrepreneurs who are not highly educated. In fact, education sometimes stands in the way of good entrepreneurship. Too much thinking and reasoning are not always helpful in making good decisions. Good entrepreneurship also requires intuition. Intuition has to do with unconsciously stored experiences. You know how to do and solve things without being able to consciously reason. It's a kind of sixth sense by which you know things without knowing how you know them. Good and healthy intuition is an important quality for entrepreneurs.

Working on Excellence

Excellence has to do with distinguishing yourself in the business world by providing a high-quality service. This has nothing to do with political maneuvering and manipulation; it is all about serving those with whom you work to make the surroundings around you a better place for all.

If you are captivated by God's love, you want to give back the best of the skills and talents you've been given by God to serve humanity and society. By making the most of your talents, you honor God, showing the world that you are grateful for what you have received. As the Olympian sprinter Eric Liddell from the film *Chariots of Fire* says, "God made me fast. When I run, I feel his pleasure." God enjoys it when we work with what he has given us. He calls us to develop our talents, our personality, our

IQ, and everything else we've been given. Putting to good use what God has given us is something God will measure on his final judgment.[2]

To become Christian entrepreneurs of excellence, we must ask ourselves, *Have I done everything I can to the best of my abilities? If so, I will give it to God. If not, I then will go back and will get (my part of) the job done.*

Excellence and Efficiency

How do excellence and efficiency relate to each other? They are not mutually exclusive. On the contrary, they reinforce each other. In every company, there are regular discussions about cost savings. Traditional cost savings often manifest themselves in the reduction of direct costs. This can include lowering salaries, squeezing out suppliers, or reducing the amount of product in the packaging by a small percentage without attracting attention. In that case, it is not improvements that are being made, but it is depreciating the value. Instead of saving by limiting services provided, you can also work on preventing avoidable costs. You can work better and more efficiently. A better process adds value to the business and the product, while flat cost savings often remove the added value. This is a saving that takes costs out of the organization instead of taking money away from the client.

Striving for excellence and efficiency is striving for improvement—improvement that leads to less waste, fewer failure costs, more revenue, and better service. An operational management focused on excellence works on high-quality and efficient service in order to better serve the client. The spin-off is a higher yield. A good example is the hospitality branch. Excellence in this branch was often mixed up with more luxury, more staff, and more costs. Nowadays, we see that luxury has nothing to do with over-the-top bling or more expenses, but with good quality that is sustainable, environmentally friendly, aesthetically good looking, and distinct. Less is more. It is about quality, not about the price or expenses.

The same is true with personal attention. Personal attention is not having more staff but serving with a smile, letting people feel that they are seen and valued, working on efficiency in order to cut the lines of waiting, and doing your job without failures, in time, and fast. This is more valued than having people available for unnecessary services. Lean working is excellent and efficient.

In leadership, excellence is about the transformational, servant, and authentic aspects of a leader. Transformation can occur through encouragement and teamwork but also through high-performance targets and encouraging people to think out of the box. The servant aspect of the leader is about showing interest and empathy, helping people to find their right place to work, placing them in a motivational environment (which can also be outside the company), and offering empowerment throughout the experience.

Authentic leaders are willing to learn, understanding they are work in progress too and being able to work on reverse mentoring, where both sides benefit. They are free of passing judgments but are curious and ask questions to work on improving skills and talents. Authentic leaders who walk the talk, who live their values, and who practice their calling in daily life are highly appreciated and receive authority because of who they are.

Excellence within the current generation of young professionals is sparked by a shared vision, dream, and purpose, where everyone is equal in value, but all have different roles. When employees can visibly contribute to the mission and vision of the company, they feel attracted to and can show up at their work with their whole self.

On the financial side, this all leads to increased revenue through lower costs, better performance, higher prices, and higher margins. Fewer failures result in less waste and fewer failure costs. On the social and relational side, we have higher revenues because the client is more satisfied with our excellent services. As a result, we have higher client satisfaction, more returning clients, a better image, and an outstanding reputation. This, in turn, leads to a reduction in marketing and acquisition costs.

High-quality service, excellent client satisfaction, and more profit lead to a feeling of satisfaction, purpose, and meaning among the staff and the entrepreneur. Excellence also stimulates the spiritual side. We honor God because we prevent waste and thereby sustain creation. We honor God because we have servant-hearted people at the heart of our business operations. We also honor God because, with the trademark of excellence, we are a reflection of him as people created in his image and likeness. Excellence leads to profit in all areas of life and business success.

Qualities of a Christian Jerusalem Entrepreneur

Entrepreneurship requires various entrepreneurial skills, but a Christian Jerusalem entrepreneur also has a special set of qualities. I would like to look at the character of two great kings who ruled Jerusalem: David and Solomon. Some of these qualities are mentioned in the list above, but those of David and Solomon have a specific Jerusalem dimension.

These are David and Solomon's qualities, which also help define the Christian Jerusalem entrepreneur:

- A leader after God's heart (David)
- Courageous and competent (David)
- Defeats the enemies of good (David)
- Wisdom and insight (Solomon)

A Leader After God's Own Heart

Even though David made many mistakes and did some terrible things (like adultery and murder), he was still called a man after God's heart.[3] What does one need to receive this description? It is someone who lives by faith, who is willing to be held accountable, and who is teachable. David was such a man, a man with the heart to serve and to listen to God, which set him apart from his predecessor, Saul, who wanted to live his own life.

Saul failed to seek God for who God is. He didn't love God, but feared God, and was looking for God's favor to become personally successful. Like many Babylonian-motivated leaders, he was primarily focused on himself and his own interests. This self-centeredness played tricks on Saul at crucial moments and negatively influenced his decisions. As a result, he lost God's favor.[4] David stayed connected to God because he loved God,[5] desiring to dedicate his life and kingship to God.

From David's example, we see that a leader after God's heart lives in *intimacy* with God, he *trusts* God's intentions, he lives in *accountability* to God, and he wants to *continuously improve*, becoming the kind of man God intended.

Intimacy

David loves God and continuously seeks intimacy with him, just as someone in love is constantly looking for time with his or her beloved. David writes many psalms about this.[6]

This connection with God is our lifeline. Through this connection, God is able to speak about our business and our decisions. And out of this intimacy, we receive comfort in times of crisis. Many people ask me what the added value of Christianity is for an entrepreneur in times of crisis. In most cases, I reply with the following arguments.

When my company goes through a difficult time, it makes a huge difference if I am going through this difficulty by myself or with someone else. In this intimacy with God, I have someone I can talk to, cry to, ask for advice, and even fight with. I can pray to God and receive advice. Out of this daily intimacy, I have recognized how God can work in my life and business. I understand his power and presence in this world, and this understanding helps me to stay secure in current crises. It provides trust. I am also more aware of his promises and character, which helps me to understand that every end has a new beginning.

In times of crisis, I don't have to fear that I may lose something. I can always rebuild and start to work in a better way. His promises provide a great perspective. I can see how difficulties outside of this intimate relationship are opportunities to grow. I can receive inner peace and a clear mind because I know I am embedded in his favor, even when I am out of control. Out of this intimacy grows a living relationship with the almighty God who comforts me and helps me as an entrepreneur. This can be true for you, as well.

Without this, we can talk about God but not to him. We cannot know God from personal experience. Without this intimacy, we may have our own thoughts and opinions about daily life and business, as well as about God and Jesus, but we do not share in his thoughts. If God cannot reveal himself to you because you are too busy, how will you know his thoughts about your business? God wants to speak to us and reveal who he is and how that will bless us. This is his heart's desire.[7]

Jesus said, "Abide in me, and I in you...Whoever abides in me and I in him, he it is that bears much fruit, for apart from me you can do nothing... I have called you friends, for all that I have heard from my Father I have made known to you..."[8]

Trusting God's Intentions

The keyword for belief in the Old Testament is *aman*. The primary meaning of this word is "to rely on" or "to entrust oneself to." The Greek equivalent is *pisteuein* and expresses "trust" or "having faith in." Faith and trust are synonyms. The Bible, God, and Jesus all call upon us to trust them so that they may care for us. David knows this kind of trust in God and speaks of it often in the Psalms. He sees God as his shepherd who will take care of him.[9] God is his refuge, a fortress.[10] God is a hiding place for David, with whom he is safe.[11] He is a shelter,[12] someone who protects and saves you. God is someone who watches over your life[13] and is always near.[14] David has faith in God and entrusts himself to God.[15]

Trust is necessary to make good decisions. For good business decisions, we need to have inner peace and a clear mind. Knowing that God is with us enables us to take risks and helps us survive uncertain situations. I have to think of Jane, who had to close her company because her business concept didn't work anymore. But her dream and entrepreneurial spirit didn't die. She loves to share the gospel and work for a fair, righteous, and sustainable society. So she started selling clothing online—made without using child labor, without exploitation, and without extremely long working days.

In addition, she wanted to only use environmentally friendly production processes. She wanted people to wear fashionable, attractive, and fair clothes that would make them feel good about themselves. Because of her trust in God and her holy discontent about injustice in the clothing industry, she started again with the help of good friends. Now she is back on track. Losing the company did not impact her trust because she didn't believe in herself but in God, who put this calling for clothing people well on her heart.

Trust grows through experience and time and must be earned. Trust is sometimes under pressure because we expect God to behave differently when we face bankruptcy or difficult business situations. The question that arises at these moments is this: *What can and can't we expect from God?* Too often our picture of God is shaped by our upbringing, culture, and the words we hear. This puts people's trust in God under pressure.

An example that illustrates this is a story about my good friend John, who once was going to be bankrupt. He was afraid, desperate, and accused God, saying that he didn't provide for his needs and had treated him wrongly. But when we took a closer look at his business together, we discovered that his business was not sustainable anymore. His business model was obsolete. He did not change his behavior and model, even though the demands in society were changing and his competitors picked up on those changes.

He explained later how this bankruptcy was God's megaphone to give him a last warning: "Watch out, for your business is going in a bad direction. Change now, for it is not too late." If we see God as a nice grandfather who always gives his grandchildren what they long for, we have a wrong idea about him. God is our Father who desires to grow us to maturity, and part of that is showing us how to solve our own problems.

David's trust in God often involves being in conflict with God. He sees things happening around him that don't match his image of who God is. He expected a different outcome. This may have affected David's expectations, but not his trust. In this wrestling between expectations and trust, he called upon God as the one he could trust. He asked God for help and insight, confident that God would answer him. Psalm 27 is a beautiful example of this. This trust characterizes his existence.

Do we dare entrust ourselves to God in our business lives, or do we as entrepreneurs think that we have a better understanding of entrepreneurship and leave the church to God? If our faith is limited to subscribing to the dogmas of the church, then we miss the essence of the faith.

Improvement Through Accountability

We're all people in progress. Nobody is perfect, not even David. Although he was a man after God's heart, he had his own human shortcomings. The greatest drama of his life was sleeping with the wife of Uriah.[16] Uriah was one of his heroes, and probably also a friend.[17] David had Uriah murdered in cold blood to take his wife and conceal his own adultery.[18] What's unique about David is that he finally admitted his wrongdoing, repented, and accepted the consequences. He had friends who keep him accountable, like Nathan the prophet, who confronted him about Uriah.

Do we have fellow Christian entrepreneurs to whom we can and want to be accountable? I am part of a group of Christian entrepreneurs in my hometown. We call it an accountability group and it is facilitated by CBMC (a global movement of Christian businesspeople). In this group, we share life, pray for each other, help each other, and advise each other. Together we launch activities to share the gospel and bless the local city. We also help each other do this at a personal and company level.

For me and for my business, this group is incredibly important because I can share my failures, doubts, vulnerability, and mistakes, as well as the decisions I have to make. The group is safe. These people understand me and speak God's truth into my life and business. These friends hold me accountable, and by their wisdom, I can improve my life and business. I see them as a part of God's voice in my life, just as Nathan was in David's life.

Courageous and Competent

David was brave because he knew God was with him.[19] He was not courageous because he ignored the danger. His courage was about stepping into dangerous situations with awareness. His courage was entering into the unknown or speaking up for someone else, possibly at the expense of his own life, as we saw in the way he approached Goliath. He spoke up for Israel and for God. David combined courage with trust in God, which is a powerful combination. This trust in God gave him the courage to be able to act in matters of injustice and to fight for good. We as Christian entrepreneurs should do so as well. Do we speak on behalf of our leadership? What battles do we choose to fight within our businesses and personal lives? Do we fight a corrupt society and a tough and ruthless business culture?

Making choices and daring to stand up at the right times takes courage. My friend Slava does this. He lives in a poor country in eastern Europe; many of his friends have left the nation and gone to western Europe or the US to have a better life. But not Slava. With his knowledge about EU food requirements and regulations, he stays in this nation to help small farmers in remote areas gain access to the European markets. He serves them with microcredit, which he can provide because of his relationships with the richer part of Europe. He helps these farmers with his knowledge about agriculture. In this way, he is fighting the unjust system in his nation and provides for the needs of the local village people. He is brave enough to stay and make a change for the better, even though he has had plenty of opportunities to establish a wealthy and easy life in western Europe or the States.

Back to David. Not only was he brave, but he was also competent as a king to lead his people with a capable hand. He established a good government. This combination of competence and courage makes him particularly powerful in executing his role as king. I see that same powerful combination in the life of my friend Slava.

Defeating the Enemies of Good

Good is never meant to be taken for granted. Enemies exist. We have internal enemies, such as our distorted longings and desires, our ego, and our desire for recognition and status. These sometimes drive us into regretful situations and events that do not promote the "fullness of life." Think of adultery, lies, blackmail, power abuse, or breaking the law for business gain. We also have external enemies—others who want to rule over us and who represent evil. Think of leaders and bosses who demand things from us that are unethical. Think of a culture of doing business where our top priority is success with lawsuits, manipulation, and political games.

Good is being cultivated by our human efforts and by our *spiritual health*. The more we do this, the more evil is forced to withdraw from our lives. David asks for a *pure* heart and a *renewal* of the mind,[20] realizing that the heart is the source of action. Our deepest desires and ambitions determine our thinking and actions. Our actions determine who we are and our future. If we want to fight evil, we must first make our hearts right.

One of our most important tasks as human beings is to be the gatekeeper of our hearts. The heart is influenced by what we allow inside, so we must protect our hearts by being particular about this. We do this by choosing what deals we make and what we know to be dubious, the boundaries we make between work and home, and how we treat those around us. We do this by choosing what we do and do not read, and who we want to deal with and who we do not. Everything we see, hear, and do—and also the environment in which we live—influences how we live and treat our employees, clients, or colleagues.

It's important to be perceptive and not accept everything blindly. Jesus says, "I am sending you out as sheep in the midst of wolves, so be wise as serpents and innocent as doves."[21] Solomon says, "Keep your heart with all vigilance, for from it flow the springs of life."[22]

David's struggle against the Philistines, his external enemies, lasted his entire life. Our fight against evil will also take up our entire lives. We try to promote good by the choices we make each day and by the way we live even though we're surrounded by a culture that is not necessarily good. This means that we're asked to stand up for those unable to speak or for people who remain marginalized. Because of our natural position as entrepreneurs, we can use our businesses to do so.

A great example of this is Tony Chocolonely, who has been working toward making all chocolate 100% slave free.[23] It all started with the holy discontent of a journalist, Teun van de Keuken, who was shocked when he read a book about illegal child labor and modern slavery on cocoa farms in West Africa. Out of this holy discontent, he started to make a series of chocolate bars to prove to the industry that it is possible to produce them without using child labor.

The chocolate bars became a huge success, and the demand became so high that a company was born. Their company goal is not only to produce slave-free chocolate bars but also for the entire global chocolate industry to become 100% slave-free. They are the top national chocolate brand in the Netherlands and are starting to have an impact internationally, as well.[24]

The best way to fight evil is not always a simple act of resistance. Peter and Paul point in another direction—to fighting evil by doing the right thing.[25] "Do not be overcome by evil, but overcome evil with good."[26] Fighting evil with evil only leads to more of it. Being an example of doing good may inspire people. In letting the good grow by doing the good, the good person proves himself and challenges the other person by comparison.

I would also like to draw attention to Paul's argument in Ephesians 6:10-20. He does not consider this fight a fight against people, but a fight *for* the good and *against* evil. It is much more a battle against heavenly principalities, against the rulers of darkness, and against the evil spirits in the heavenly realms.

Although we're fighting a spiritual battle, the weapons he shows us are simple, down to earth, and very useful. They are:

- Speaking and doing the truth
- Practicing justice
- Engaging the gospel of peace
- Relying on God

- Realizing the power of your identity in Christ as a redeemed and liberated believer
- Receiving the Bible and the Holy Spirit
- Praying

A fitting example of this is Graham Power, a Christian entrepreneur famous for his focus on prayer. Graham is the owner of the Power group of companies.[27] For a large number of years, they have lived up to their purpose[28] to "improve the quality of life in Africa" through infrastructure development. Through the Unashamedly Ethical initiative, Graham Power is challenging individuals and businesses across the world to be ethical and a force for good in all their dealings and actions.[29] Graham states, "Time itself does not change things. People change things–over time. Our initiatives spur actions. Actions that trigger events that shape the future: for ourselves and for those whose lives crossed our path."

Wisdom

Next to God, the foundation of a good life, as Solomon sees it, is wisdom. Wisdom is a gift from God, which develops through reflection and contemplation.[30] Wisdom protects you from bad decisions, from evil, and from going down the wrong path. Wisdom is therefore worth more than gold, including knowledge and status.[31]

Solomon has recorded these wisdom experiences in proverbs, poems, and stories in a collection of work called the *wisdom literature* of the Bible.

As an entrepreneur, I urge you to take this wisdom seriously. Study it! I also plead for more teaching of this wisdom literature in schools and universities because wisdom helps you succeed in real ways. I learned from the book of Ecclesiastes how money, fame, and greatness are relative.[32] This clicked with my personal experience, having discovered how being successful and wealthy is of less value than bearing fruit for God and taking care of the people around me. In the end, I felt more successful and I served people with my company with profit as a result. Another example of biblical wisdom is the teaching that laziness leads to poverty and zealous work to prosperity.[33] My parents taught me this principle from the book of Proverbs, and I still profit from it.

Yet another biblical example of wisdom is about insight into investments: "Cast your bread upon the waters, for you will find it after many days. Give a portion to seven, or even to eight, for you know not what disaster may happen on earth."[34] This is advice to invest in good opportunities, for they will pay off someday. Moreover, it is important to invest in a variety of different branches and investment possibilities because you never know for sure which will flourish and which will yield less.

Wisdom provides prosperity, knowledge, and insight. This makes it possible for you to fulfill your calling in a good way. For me, in addition to professional skills, wisdom and insight are among the most important core qualities of a good leader.

Sure, we also need to be competent in carrying out and completing our tasks. But without wisdom and insight, all knowledge is useless and leads us in the wrong direction. To quote Steven Covey, "If the ladder is not leaning against the right wall, every step we take just gets us to the wrong place faster."[35] Wisdom and insight point knowledge and skills in the right direction so that the right goals are achieved.

We currently live in a society with access to more information, more possibilities, and more technology than ever before. Yet we often miss the insight and wisdom to make all of this fruitful for humans in a way that creates "life to the full."

9

Creating Well-Being

The fourth characteristic of the Christian Jerusalem entrepreneur is that his work creates well-being. A great example of this is a friend of mine. He wants his companies to be a source of well-being and he works at this on every level in his company. His companies' operations are environmentally friendly. He invests in the local community by providing a community house, social welfare, and other benefits that are not provided by the government. He pays attention to his staff and their personal needs; he enables his staff to support the needs of the region. In this way, he receives a lot of goodwill and people like to work for him and his company. His staff is highly motivated and really believes what he believes about this world. His staff sees his company as their own way of contributing to society and its well-being.

In his commercial business, he also contributes to well-being because he is in interior design. He wants people to feel well. This showed a while ago when he had a huge argument with his logistic partner. This partner was using cheap drivers from abroad. They were cheap because their working conditions were terrible. They did not have good sleeping places and were paid very poorly. My friend calculated the costs and benefits of improving the working conditions and concluded that it was financially possible. He then urged his logistic partner to make it happen. Today, these drivers have good sleeping places, drive regular hours, and can travel regularly to their families abroad.

To create well-being, the entrepreneur must act justly toward his fellow man, toward God, and toward creation. Justice and righteousness are the foundation of God's reign[1] and, therefore, of well-being. On the new earth, all things will soon be made right and their purposes will be fulfilled. Creation, human dignity, and existing structures will be restored so that there is peace, abundance, and well-being. Man will fulfill his task as the steward of creation to his original calling with Jesus, the cornerstone.

This task of stewarding God's world was there from creation, is there now, and will continue to be there in the future. We as Christian Jerusalem entrepreneurs must be aligned with God's longing and vision for this world. It must become ours as we contribute to this with all our efforts and endeavors. Our skills and our companies are the primary means to contribute to this.

The work of the Christian Jerusalem entrepreneur is linked to this future perspective; he desires to bring that perspective into the present. As Jesus prayed and taught us to pray, "Let your will be done on Earth as in Heaven."

As we saw in the previous chapters, God equips everyone, including entrepreneurs, with specific qualities, talents, and skills. Nimrod used these qualities for himself and for building his own kingdom. The prostitute of Babylon saw these qualities as opportunities to become rich and gain influence and power. She constructed a perfect paradise for herself, and she views this paradise as well-being in optimal form. In this way, she is violating God's order and thoughts about well-being.

God is the opposite. He gives himself, his glory, and his splendor to the city of Jerusalem and its people. He does not dress in beautiful and expensive garments but clothes his people in beautiful and expensive garments. He dresses them in white garments, representing all the good and righteous deeds that God has enabled his people to do.[2]

Christian Jerusalem entrepreneurs are called to live and work according to God's character. Depending on the circumstances, there are different possibilities for us as entrepreneurs to contribute to well-being. Below, I will discuss a few business models to help you discover how you can create well-being and live as a Christian Jerusalem entrepreneur.

Profit is a result.

In a healthy business model, the client is central. Suppose someone has a need. If I am a smart entrepreneur, businessman, or particularly gifted craftsman, I can provide for this need or desire. That's why I develop a product or service and sell it to the client. The wishes of the client are the starting point of my actions; his satisfaction in having his needs met is my goal. My service or product is a means to meet the needs of the client and satisfy him.

The Client	The Product and Service	Profit
The *goal* and purpose of the business or company	The *means* to serve the client	The *result*

The compensation we receive for this service is more than its costs, a difference we call profit, which is the result of good service and management. Healthy numbers are a basic requirement for a sustainable company. We need both profits and a positive result to live on. We must be able to continue to invest in research and development, in new opportunities, in new projects, and in new businesses. We must be able to save for old age and illness. We need reserves for the bad years because they will come. We pay tax from our profits. In this way, we contribute to the well-being of the society in which we operate. We pay dividends to shareholders who finance businesses and make it possible to operate our business. A good and healthy profit makes all kinds of good things possible and justifies the existence of the company. However, profit is never an end in itself. It both *has* a function and *is* a result.

The Client as an ATM

Instead of justice, the focus of Babylon (and most of the business world) is exclusively getting rich. In fact, this is the starting point of many an entrepreneur and company. Shareholder value is the deciding factor. Of course, profit plays an important role. After all, companies operate in an economic environment and need profits to continue existing. Nevertheless, a single focus on profit maximization quickly leads to all kinds of undesirable behavior. I will make this clear with the following models:

Profit	**The Client**	**The Product and Service**
Has become the *goal*	Has become the *means*	Have become the *costs*

There are plenty of examples. Think of fiddling with emission requirements, as some big car companies did, to meet the tests which measure carbon dioxide emissions levels. They had implemented a "defeat device" in engines that could detect when they were being tested, changing the performance accordingly to improve results.[3] Another example is the melamine scandal, where high levels of the dangerous industrial chemical melamine were added to powdered baby milk so that it would appear as if there was enough protein. That milk made babies and children sick and resulted in deaths.[4]

Think also of certain pharmaceutical businesses that buy up other businesses to create a monopoly and therefore increase the price of medicine. Some of these businesses even close down their Research and Development departments. The turnover and profits of these types of businesses are skyrocketing. Soon, the business becomes the darling of the stock market and the CEO gets the glory and bonuses that they long for. Other extreme examples include forms of child labor and new forms of the slave trade in which the exploitation of minors from poor countries plays a role.

When profits become the goal, client satisfaction is no longer the main focus—making money is. We begin to see the client as an ATM, as an instrument for profit, but no longer as a person we can help with our service and services. People then shift from the purpose to something seen as a means to the ultimate goal of profit.

If the client only means profit, then the product or our services are no longer so important. The only reason we pay attention to a product or service is to sell it. As long as we can sell the service or the product, everything is fine. The well-being of the client is no longer the inspiration or even of secondary importance. An example of this in business is the selling of unnecessary insurance policies in which fear is used as a motive for purchase but does not actually benefit the client.

Sometimes, in this mentality, the quality of the service of the product is also reduced, but as long as we remain within the agreed principles, legal frameworks, and standards, everything is permitted in the thinking of "profit first." For example, infrastructural works or ICT (information communications technology) projects can be carried out in such a way that there is an inferior product made or a substantial cost is overrun though the builder was already aware of this at the time of signing. Contracts are scanned by the legal department to enable additional work and extra revenue afterward.

It is possible that we cut back so much on the cost of a product that the quality at a given moment no longer meets what is required. Sometimes there is deliberate fraud and we end up doing something illegal. In this way of thinking, the client and the service have no intrinsic value; the only value is in relation to the profit and the profit figure.

Searching for Alternatives

A question I'm often asked is, "Can we use the first model (with the client at the center) and still beat the competition with pressure on prices and survive a crisis?" Even when, as suppliers, we experience price pressure from our clients, there are other solutions besides lowering the quality of our product or services for cost savings. As suppliers, we can avoid price pressure by innovation—by adding value instead of taking it away.

During the 2009–2014 economic crisis, the general contractors in the construction industry in the Netherlands were surviving by using very Babylonian thinking; they were putting pressure on subcontractors and exploiting them. Many general contractors abused their power by using their position in the supply chain to renegotiate rates. Sometimes they did not pay the final invoices. They threatened lawsuits. The subcontractors had to tighten their belts and hope that it would turn out in the end.

The legal departments of the general contractors grew. A new revenue model was the exploration of the specifications and requirements in a tender for errors. If errors were found, they offered lower prices and the profit was secured through additional work. Building on the service to the client was no longer the earning model; the legal calculation of the specifications and the renegotiation of the price with subcontractors and suppliers became the new focus.

However, in these difficult times, there were also positive exceptions that used Jerusalem thinking and focused on increasing value and quality. I spoke to a building contractor who, during this crisis, invited his subcontractors and suppliers to think along with him in the process of pricing in the projects as early as the architectural stage of the project. They were looking for alternative ways of designing, manufacturing, and working more efficiently. They created new solutions. This collaboration resulted in lower costs because unnecessary costs and failure costs were actually avoided. In addition to lower costs, the results were often of higher quality. In the middle of a crisis, this contractor managed to lower his prices, expand his market share, and recreate and improve the quality of the products. Pressure and setbacks led to an overall improvement.

We must be aware of the culture we're creating when we allow Babylon thinking. "Small" acts or decisions become examples for the industry and create a ripple effect. Personnel takes on the boss's behavior.[5] Clever tricks become habits and people justify themselves by comparing their actions to the behavior of others. Which world are our actions building up? A small transgression is often bigger than it seems because it leads to a cultural change. The world of construction in the Netherlands will never be the same because of 2008. Because of the crisis, definite changes have become absorbed into the cultural mentality. Some see this as beneficial, others as a loss.

Corporate Social Responsibility

If well-being is our starting point and our primary driver, and if the pursuit of justice and righteousness (so that everything is as it is designed to be by God) is the foundation of well-being, how should we view the model of corporate social responsibility?

Corporate social responsibility (CSR) is a type of international private business self-regulation that aims to contribute to the societal goals of a philanthropic, activist, or charitable nature by engaging in or supporting ethically-oriented practices.[6] In the case of CSR, we strive for social goals and well-being, but to achieve these goals, the financial objectives are still the starting point. See the picture below.

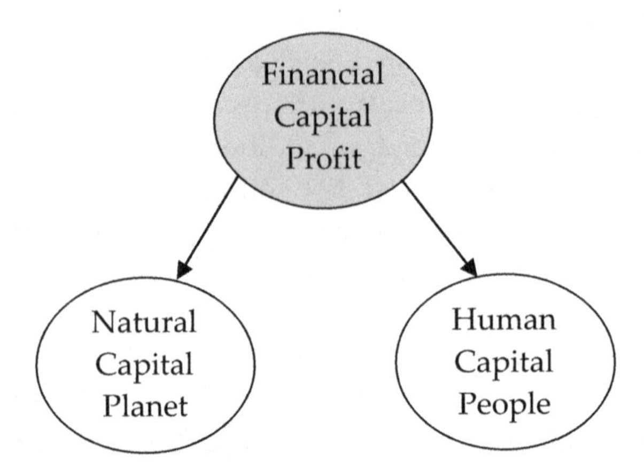

The financial outcome of the company defines its possibilities. The investment in the well-being of people and creation depends on the profit the company is making. Less profit equals less investment. It is not the company itself and the purpose of the company that drives this model for well-being.

CSR is still driven by the financial outcome of business. Investments in well-being or people and creation are defined by how large the company's profit is. Therefore, this investment can be greater or smaller. It is not anchored in the purpose of the company or its processes. Many times, it is only used to contribute to a brand's reputation. In this way, it is a Babylonian system in disguise (although many companies have an honorable attitude).

A good and admirable example of CSR is the company Bosch, which has a turnover of $78 billion and EBIT[7] of $5.3 billion.[8] A foundation owns this company, which forever focuses on the development of social capital.[9] In some foundations owned by businesses or companies, other businesses also participate to gain more clout. An example of this is a "small" foundation, such as the Focusplaza Foundation.[10] This foundation focuses on the social and economic improvement of the poorest people in African countries regardless of their background or religion. Focusplaza's goal is to increase the sustainability of income and self-reliance. In addition, they work with partners who invest in leadership developments to stimulate cultural change and a change in mentality.

Purpose Driven

In a company where the motive has changed from financial goals to a purpose and ideal that is greater than the existence of the business, the meaning is central. Well-being is anchored in the strategy and behavior of the company. Meaning or purpose can be defined in different ways but is usually closely related to the personal motives of the entrepreneur. In his famous TED talk, *How great leaders inspire to action*, Simon Sinek says, "People don't buy what you do, but why you do it." This indicates that the personal values of an entrepreneur or a company can become a model for revenue or USP.[11] I know from experience that this can work.

There was an entrepreneur, Paul, who was driven by a striving for perfection. His life motto was that things had to be true and honest. He strived for the highest possible quality and always delivered on time, as agreed. Paul worked concrete, a commodity and sector where it's difficult to distinguish yourself from your competitors. He wasn't the cheapest, but he was doing well.

When he was asked why his clients bought from him even though he was using a higher price in a transparent market of raw materials and semi-finished products, he didn't really know. As a perfectionist, Paul thought this was a good question, so he went to investigate. He called several clients and visited his most important clients personally.

What was the result? Almost all his clients bought from him because he was always on time and because everything was always right. Most of them knew that as an owner, he was a perfectionist and strived for the highest quality. This gave them the guarantee that everything was executed perfectly, as agreed. He always delivered on time. This was important to them because the clients could not afford delays, extra stock, or extra costs. The invoicing was digitally linked to the delivery note that the client agreed to and it was also always correct, so they no longer had to check the invoices.

The quality of the delivered product was consistent; they could rely on it. They weren't buying the product; they were buying Paul's personal values. At that moment, he realized that with his way of working and the example he was giving, he could sell any product. His personal beliefs were the basis of his success.

A fitting example of a purpose-driven company is Bambook,[12] a young, promising company where meaning is central. Four young men started their business because they wanted to reduce paper waste. They now produce sustainable and reusable notebooks. The notebooks are made by disabled people in a workshop.

The distribution is done—where possible—with bicycle couriers. They work on afforestation and plant trees for every notebook sold. In the beginning, I talked to one of the founders about profit maximization, an increase in turnover, and production in China, but he didn't want to hear about it. For him and his friends, the idea behind this was to "wake up in a world without waste." Now, five years later, they are in the Innovation Top 100, are growing, have an impact, are known within the international market, and have healthy financial results. Working with purpose pays off.

In such operational management, the purpose of the company, and not the financial objectives, is central. "The need is the call," as a good friend once told me. Profit is a result, and finance is a means to an end.

Many businesses have already made this transformation. For example, IKEA formulates its objective in this way: "to create a better everyday life for the many people by offering a wide range of well-designed, functional home furnishing products at prices so low that as many people as possible will be able to afford them."[13]

Today, values such as sustainability, health, and environmentally and people-friendly production have become driving forces behind earning models. They are added to the classic values of excellence and reliability. However, these new values only work if we actually experience them. We must be who we say we are. What's important is that the production process and our business operations are based upon these very values, down to every detail, and that they also survive under financial pressure. The challenge is to stick to these values, even in difficult circumstances when the temptation to stray from them is strongest.

One bank director, for example, spoke to his staff during the banking crisis and said, "We need to reform banking by being more mindful of the interests of clients and society. We can't afford to go on like this anymore." This led to cheers and great enthusiasm from his staff. And then he concluded with, "But the main thing is and remains maximizing profit and shareholder value." Everyone in the audience knew at that moment what he meant by this closing sentence. As a result, nothing essential changed at this bank, and a scandal followed on the heels of his address.

The Purpose-Driven Mutuality Model

Some businesses go further than just making meaning the starting point of their actions. The Economics of Mutuality was developed within Mars, Incorporated, in close partnership with Oxford University. It empowers companies to adopt a responsible and more complete form of capitalism that is fairer and performs better than the purely financial version operating today. Three key ideals lie behind the Economics of Mutuality:

- The primacy of purpose in driving strategy
- The power of orchestrating ecosystems at the business unit level around the purpose to mobilize and enhance hitherto untapped resources and value
- The importance of enhancing management accounting across multiple forms of capital—social, human, natural, and shared financial—to drive holistic value creation[14]

For the purpose of this book, it is important to understand the concept of the multiplication of different forms of capital and how they interact and make each other stronger. We call this the *economics of mutuality*.[15]

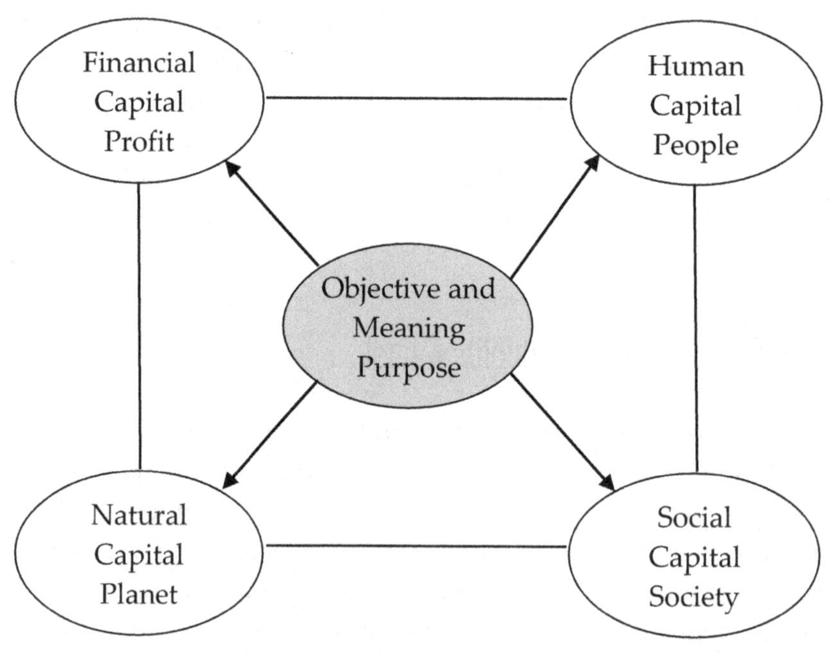

A company that is driven by meaning and wants to multiply different types of capital.

The point here is not only that meaning is the starting point and earning model, but also that value is added to all forms of capital by what actions businesses take. As you can see, the various forms of capital reinforce each other and are interdependent. Author Bruno Roche distinguishes four different types of capital in his book, *Completing Capitalism:* human capital (the individual person), social capital (society), natural capital (creation and raw materials), and financial capital.[16] For a company to add value to all types of capital, we need measurable and manageable indicators.

Mutuality and Interaction

The challenge for the Christian entrepreneur is to allow these types of capital (including the not yet mentioned spiritual capital) to mutually strengthen each other from the core values this company is centered on. When we invest in one part of these forms of capital, the other parts will be mutually strengthened as well. This gives us a more holistic approach to our company and makes a well-lived life more possible. This mutuality makes life fuller, more beautiful, and more abundant. It gives joy and meaning.

Human Capital

Let's take a closer look at the different forms of capital. First, we have human capital, which is about the individual well-being of various people in the company. Working on human capital means working on the social cohesion in business and the extent to which objectives can be worked on within the teams. The focus is on reducing absenteeism due to workplace fatigue or injury, working on resilience, providing more and better training, and creating internal promotional opportunities and opportunities for personal development. It can also be about one's own initiative to be involved in the meaning of business and its objectives.

Important indicators for the well-being of the staff are leaders who walk the talk, prospects of upward mobility, social cohesion, being seen and heard as an individual, being part of the company's solutions for internal challenges, and being attracted to the purpose of the company.

Healthy and motivated people (human capital) contribute to the development of financial capital. Healthy, well-educated, and ethically oriented people contribute to the common good. Motivated people who can connect and work together on a team have a positive influence on social capital, financial capital, and human capital. People with a sense of responsibility and vision for the future can develop and add meaning while contributing to preserving and caring for natural capital.

Investing in people is making people flourish and contributing to their well-being. Therefore, we need to pay attention to our personnel policy, among other things. The themes for well-being in modern Western economies in this respect are work pressure, stress, resilience, people's personal development, giving meaning and purpose, and living in loving relationships.

Many consumers would like companies to be open and transparent about the circumstances in which their products are being made. We also know that the well-being of employees is under pressure in many nations. Child labor and slavery are still common in various nations. In a well-led Jerusalem company, this topic needs to be addressed. Some companies use blockchain technology to help them with this. It gives unique codes to products (as well as semi-manufactured products) with a traceable origin that gives us information about the quality, labor circumstances, and structure of the product. For example, in Western countries, it is possible to scan a code that is placed on the bananas you buy in the supermarket. This code leads you to a host of information and even a movie about the production of these bananas. With this code, you know exactly from which plantation the bananas are coming and the circumstances in which they grow. This transparency gives the consumer power to enforce well-being by choosing which bananas they want to buy.

Social Capital

Social capital is about the common good. Investing in the community around us contributes to the well-being of society and of individuals.

The main benefits for society of having businesses and companies, in general, is that they create jobs, yield tax income, and cause economic development. This is also true for less privileged countries.

For example, if more people start businesses, create jobs, and spend money, society starts developing economically. Its income and purchasing power increases. This increase in purchasing power means that consumption increases. Entrepreneurs and local authorities benefit. This is seemingly common sense, but there are large and influential entrepreneurs and leaders of countries who are only concerned with harvesting, not with sowing and fertilizing. They don't allow competitors to come to the market. They block innovation and new business models, try to keep the power by creating monopolies, and hamper new initiatives from coming to the market.

In countries where a strong elite of businesspeople control society, the country becomes poorer, the well-educated people emigrate, and the purchasing power decreases. These rich entrepreneurs and leaders go abroad with their capital to make money and multiply their capital in the international financial economy. Meanwhile, they could have used their capital to make large investments within their country, where the financial capital could have had a greater impact. They themselves would also benefit from this in the long run. In discussions, they understand this option and admit that this could be the right way forward, but then choose the short-term return.

As Jerusalem entrepreneurs, how can we contribute to the social capital through our business operations? We can do this by sharing knowledge and expertise to help people to build their own businesses. One example is a kind of (micro)franchise formula, in which people are given entrepreneurial opportunities. The formula can contribute to the community by a company providing for the needs of the community. Additionally, the business generates income, self-confidence, and development opportunities for its employees. It helps people out of poverty and, thus, gives opportunities to their children.

The franchise helps the parent company financially by expanding its market. The franchise formula also gives us insight into how business is run and enables us to draw up regulations on waste and the use of materials. In this way, value is added to the various forms of capital and we can develop less developed societies while growing the original company.

Another way we can create employment and income locally is by processing raw materials into a final product at the very place where they are extracted. Too often, we still see governments exporting raw materials and buying expensive final products. Consider a country that sells oil but has no refineries. The country sells cheap oil while importing expensive gasoline. It lacks employment and taxes and develops a one-sided and dependent economy that is sensitive to price fluctuations. I read about poor countries with sufficient agricultural land that lease their lands to other countries. The local population is hungry, yet the government buys expensive food from the land they have leased out. Instead of renting out the land, they could supply the end product to the users who need it. In this way, they create both the economy and employment. The short-term self-interest of making money now makes too many managers blind to the long-term interest of the land of business.

When the nations appear before God's throne during the final judgment, the people will be judged on their dealings with their marginalized fellow human beings.[17] The extent to which we as human beings care for those most vulnerable in our society is the assessment criterion. In the past, I thought that caring for the poor and underprivileged was called charity. First, we get rich ourselves, and then we give away the money. Nowadays, I realize it's better to promote healthy, holistic, economic development so that people can work and provide for themselves.

This is why it's so important to establish businesses and give people work. A healthy economy with the healthy participation of all its inhabitants is the fastest and best way to fulfill the mission of Jesus[18] to care for those who are naked, who thirst, and who are hungry. A healthy economy also allows us to invest in infrastructure, schools, hospitals, refugees, and rehabilitation programs for those in jail. In this way, we can use our business activities to fulfill the mission laid out in Matthew 25 by putting our economic mindset into a larger social context instead of keeping our wealth for ourselves.

Natural Capital

Natural capital is about the well-being of creation. It is about the use of raw materials and commodities and what we leave behind as waste. Many times, taking care of creation is defined in a company's output (for example, the production and reduction of CO^2 and other pollutants). In addition to focusing on the output of carbon dioxide, pollution, and waste, various companies work on compensating measures, such as planting trees and the use of solar energy. But natural capital can also include reducing the use of raw materials such as water, healthy and fertile soil, and clean air.

Preserving natural resources through technological developments and efficient production also strengthens financial capital. The reduction of emissions has a direct impact on social capital and the welfare of the people. Human capital grows, for example, because people work in a meaningful environment, which increases their well-being and motivation. It is possible to profit in all forms by saving on the use of raw materials and producing less waste.

We can also take care of waste and save raw materials and commodities by developing a circular economy. A circular economy is an economic system of closed loops in which raw materials, components, and products lose their value as little as possible, renewable energy sources are used, and systems thinking is at the core.[19] The circular economy is a new business opportunity that contributes to the well-being of creation. Think, for example, of solar panels but also of reusing raw materials. In many industries, it is possible to make a house or car out of traceable and reusable materials. Through a blockchain and a database, we can follow every individual part of a product and find it. This means that the product can be reused or processed in the right way. This is an example of how technology can help with the theme of the well-being of creation. It is not only about focusing on using less but also on being smarter. As Jerusalem entrepreneurs, we should be at the forefront of this development. In transforming our businesses and the economy into a sustainable, circular economy, we can give practical shape to our mission as stewards of this earth.

We as Jerusalem entrepreneurs don't buy into this idea of taking care of creation for the sake of reputation, image, political pressure, or socially desirable behavior. Our concerns about creation and our efforts to invest in natural capital come from our faith. It is for God, who values his creation highly, and our own convictions about well-being that we do this. Man and creation are inextricably linked.

We see that God condemns people who have negatively impacted and damaged creation. "The nations raged, but your wrath came, and the time for the dead to be judged, and for rewarding your servants, the prophets and saints, and those who fear your name, both small and great, *and for destroying the destroyers of the earth*" (italics mine).[20]

It is because of God who created and values his own creation that creation will also share in the liberation of the earth from evil and in the glory and splendor of God, which will be present in the New Jerusalem.[21]

We need to understand that the state of creation is linked to our moral attitude and behavior. It not only matters what we *do* to creation with our consumption and production but also who we *are* morally. Creation shares in our choices and actions. We experienced this at the time of the Fall[22] and we will see it again in the future.[23] Yet it is also true for our current life and existence. Listen to the prophet Hosea's words:

> Hear the word of the Lord, O children of Israel,
> for the Lord has a controversy with the inhabitants of the land.
> There is no faithfulness or steadfast love,
> and no knowledge of God in the land;
> there is swearing, lying, murder, stealing, and committing adultery; they break all bounds, and bloodshed follows bloodshed.
> Therefore the land mourns,
> and all who dwell in it languish,
> and also the beasts of the field
> and the birds of the heavens,
> and even the fish of the sea are taken away."[24]

We as humanity influence the well-being of creation also by our moral state. If we want to care for creation, then we must also care for our fellow man, and vice versa. The choices we make in doing business influence creation in many ways. Creation is closely linked to the well-being of man and God. Therefore, we must also give creation its rightful place on earth and preserve it. It is our natural capital. This requires a sustainable and circular economy. Sustainability is not a department, but a mentality.

Financial Capital

Financial capital is not only about profit and losses, balance sheets, or cash flow overviews but also the distribution of cash flows to different forms of capital. Financial capital includes the following: the percentage of turnover allocated to human capital (i.e., salaries, education, training and development, and improvements in absenteeism); the percentage of turnover allocated to the social environment of business (i.e., purchasing from local suppliers, purchasing raw materials, taxes, sponsorship projects, investments in infrastructure and buildings); and natural capital, such as savings on the purchase of raw materials, clean air, and water (in other words, the investments in new sustainable technology for a circular economy or investments in solar energy). It is helpful to make all of the above pointedly clear in our annual reports.

It is also important to be clear by stating that there is nothing wrong with creating financial wealth and abundance; after all, it is God himself who grants wealth and prosperity. But even though profit, money, and financial abilities can be a blessing to man and society when driven by Jerusalem values, there is a dark side to money. There is a spiritual power behind money, which Jesus calls *mammon*.[25] This power can take God's rightful place[26] in the way we experience the fullness of life, with our security and future depending on what we possess. Money then becomes a goal instead of a means, or even an idol.

By this point, we have switched into a Babylonian mentality with our desire for money determining our values and business operations. We might begin to introduce terms such as profit maximization. There is nothing wrong with money as a means and resulting in a profit. Money as a goal, however, is dangerous because the spiritual power behind money then begins to control our lives. Money is a perfect servant, but money should not begin to overpower our existence.

Spiritual Capital

As Christian entrepreneurs, we have additional capital to focus on: spiritual capital.

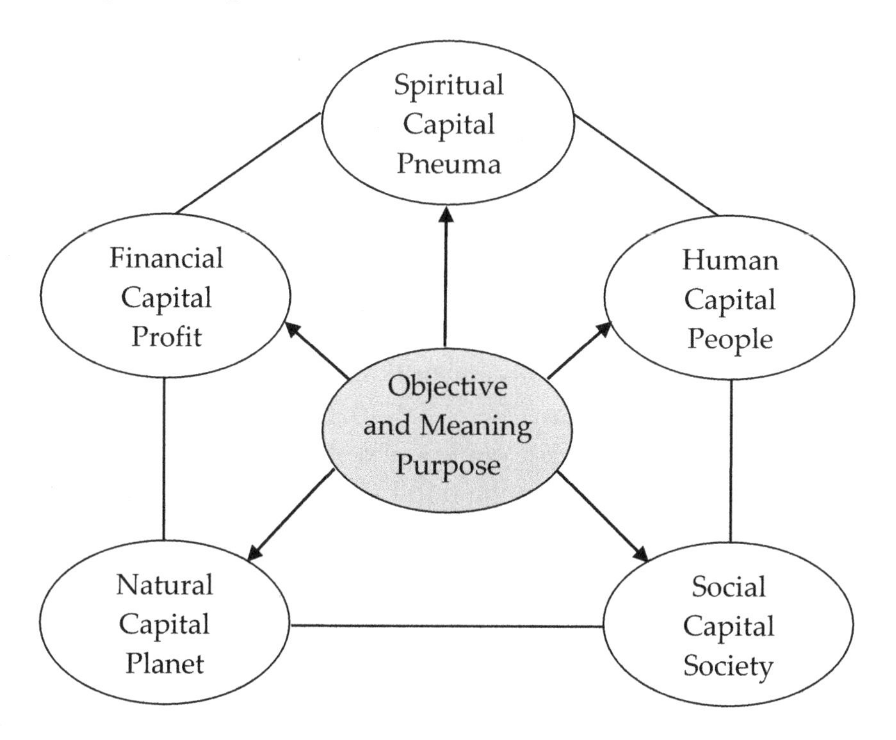

Christians should always want to work on developing spiritual capital to bring about the good news of Jesus Christ. In Babylonian culture, without Christ, developing material wealth and monetary success is the world's salvation. For a Christian entrepreneur, economic, human, and social development can never be separated from proclaiming Christ as the real salvation of the world—not as a must but as an act of love, nourished by the wonder and joy that we ourselves experience with and in Christ.

A good example of developing spiritual capital is the story of a man named Hugo, who felt called to be an entrepreneur. Hugo knew that he was good at setting up and developing businesses. This was where he found his calling and meaning. In his private holding company, his objective was to strengthen and bless the local economy by setting up various types of businesses.

He now has five major businesses in his region. He has several retail businesses, several wholesalers, and is in the middle of negotiations with a partner to set up a production company. His goal is to create employment and offer people both an income and a perspective. In this way, he builds human, social, and financial capital. He also builds spiritual capital because everyone knows that his faith is his motivation for doing business well. In addition to his own investments, he also tries to convince other businesses to invest in the region. He is in dialogue with politicians to champion good infrastructure and education. He works passionately toward his dream and manages to help all types of capital interact and grow.

Another example is Double Harvest, "a foundation that offers practical and spiritual help in Ethiopia."[27] The founders focus on multiplying multiple forms of capital in order for people to flourish. The employees on Double Harvest's farms are involved in the production of healthy food centered in Ethiopia. Since 1991, through practical help and sharing knowledge, they have been working on wonderful projects including chick hatcheries, chicken stalls, chicken slaughterhouses, a feed factory, and a milk factory. In addition, good quality vegetables are grown on a large scale and now find their way into a large part of Ethiopia. Double Harvest has constructed a school and about 20 churches. Their goal has always been to promote the well-being of all people, making the business itself a source of blessing. They want to do business from their vision, adding value to all types of capital in their business operations while each type of capital reinforces the other.

The spiritual capital is broader than one Christian testimony; it suggests growth incentives for other types of capital. By honoring and loving God with everything we have, we strive for excellence, justice, love, and life in loving relationships. These attributes guide our behaviors and policies, as well as having the added benefit of strengthening different types of capital.

Working on Well-Being

The way the various types of capital grow is determined by the choices we make when it comes to our thinking and by which spirit we allow ourselves to be guided by in our business operations.

By working from the model of meaning and adding value to all types of capital, we work toward more integrated business operations while contributing to the well-being of society. If we do this in the right way, we as entrepreneurs and companies will make a small contribution to righteousness on earth.

10

Motivation and Meaning

Recently, a supermarket cashier was asked about the meaning of her work. She answered, "I don't do this because I like to run barcodes over a scanner but because I meet people every day. A lot of older people come here every day, and they are lonely. They hope to have some contact with other people during their daily shopping. I can offer them that contact by having a chat with them. I like to talk to them because it gives me meaning, purpose, and satisfaction in my work and life."

A boy who is disabled and lives in India was locked up at home by his parents because they were ashamed of him. In the meantime, he filled his time by learning to read and write. When asked about the meaning of his existence, he replied, "I can read and write, and many other children from the village now come to me because they also want to learn to read and write. I help them with this. In this, I experience purpose and meaning."

People's well-being and God's glory is where the Christian Jerusalem entrepreneur finds his motivation and experiences meaning.[1] Much of this has been discussed in the previous chapters, but in this chapter, I want to look more at the general aspect of meaning, happiness, and well-being.

The main question is *why? Why* do we do what we do? This focuses on motivation and on the heart. The answer to the question has to do with our ambition, our dream, and our vision. In this way, *why* determines the direction in which we are going. It determines what we call success, our output, and our result. It is the driving force behind our actions.

Babylon thinkers are focused on achieving happiness and well-being through material prosperity and business success. But are these dreams and motives feasible or satisfying? What of this can we counter with a Jerusalem perspective of success and what *true* happiness and well-being are?

Thinking in Terms of Business Success

Companies in the Babylonian culture are solely guided by the need for success and results. Setbacks and failure to achieve can cause Babylonian entrepreneurs to become depressed and moody, even undermining their self-confidence in the long run, especially if their identity is linked to their company and their business success. For example, if they fail to achieve the intended results over a longer period of time, they may consider stopping and doing something else.

The reason *why* we do something must be stronger and bigger than the need to succeed. Even if success is temporarily lacking or absent, we will continue because we think we should and because doing has value in itself. The Jerusalem entrepreneur must find a purpose and goal that is bigger than himself and that makes a difference.

I know entrepreneurs in remote areas where life is less comfortable than in the cities and in industrial areas who continue to work in difficult circumstances and regions where the infrastructure is not up to standard and well-educated and equipped staff is scarce. They remain there for the people they can reach and serve and to create jobs. They keep in contact with the people they love. I don't see their company as a success in itself, but I envy their lives and mentality and consider them successful in life.

I know an experienced entrepreneur, Jack, who starts new businesses all the time, makes them successful, and then sells them. When I met him, he had just started a new business that wasn't really getting off the ground; the company's survival was hanging by a thread. The market wasn't responding, and the production numbers remained too low. He made the important discovery that his fear was not losing money but the feeling of failure if he didn't save the company. Jack discovered that business was about himself, his ambition, and his identity, and not about his calling or his answer to the question of meaning.

When he discovered that this company was about himself and his success, he began to pray and put the business in God's hands. Jack began to wonder if he should stay with it or let go of the business. On several occasions, he received confirmation that he needed to stay and pursue the success of the business, which was meaningful to Jack; apparently, this company was important to God. As a result, he continued to work, making the business successful. He survived the difficult years because he could give meaning to his work and his company. His business became a great success. If Jack hadn't had this experience, he would have stopped. He said, "It was only when I was able to let go of the success of the business as a motivation to do business that I could find the motivation to continue with the business."

The Meaning of Success?

If my sense of significance depends on the results of my work and achievements, then my emotional life quickly becomes a rollercoaster of ups and downs. If I am successful in my work, then I feel good; if I am less successful, then I feel down and miserable. For this way of life, the statement is *You are your latest success.* If the next success has a short duration, once again, you are quickly nothing. My meaning and identity are then melded with my success and my work. In this way, life becomes unpredictable, rushed, and will create dissatisfaction and discontent.

An entrepreneur named Barry once talked about his personal experience within this theme. He said, "In one very successful year, I achieved the predicted years' profit in May. Instead of celebrating, I adjusted the targets and motivated the team for a new and higher goal, which became 200% of the original year's target. In November, when the results were in, I went downhill. My wife asked me what was going on and I sadly told her that we would only make 180% of the originally forecasted annual profit." It is sad to see that Barry was unable to celebrate the fact that they still reached far over their original goal because he was allowing greater business results to define him.

The same Barry told me years later that he had changed his ambitions. He didn't want to live for business results anymore but to serve people. His profit figures and business success stay unchanged, and in addition, he experienced more enjoyment and satisfaction. When we picked up the story above, Barry said, "If I could go back to those days, I would compliment my people on what they had achieved. I would encourage them to serve more people because every person counts. In November, I would be proud and happy that we were able to deliver such a performance. Living from these values puts life into balance and gives me more satisfaction."

Finding Meaning in Values

Long-term satisfaction does not come from concrete goals defined in outcomes and positions. *Who* we are and *how* we want to live has nothing to do with circumstances, position, role, or income. That is why it is important to define our ambitions and goals of life in terms of *values* and *being*. How we want to live can be expressed in certain values or principles which form the basis of our actions and lives. Examples of these are:

- I want to live a life defined by love.
- I want my life to be determined by justice.
- Wherever I am, I want to be a person of peace.
- I want to live well in relation to myself, others, and my environment.

The values from which we want to live are our guiding principles. They define whether we will be successful Jerusalem entrepreneurs. Defining our ambition in values—not in results—makes life more beautiful and consistent. It also helps us deal with setbacks and makes us more resilient.

Personal Happiness and Well-Being

For the Christian entrepreneur, personal happiness and well-being are not found in material fortune, but in loving relationships—especially in a relationship with God and Jesus. I know a wealthy entrepreneur, Gareth, who used to own many nightclubs and casinos. He had plenty of money and could afford anything. He lived in a world of money, women, alcohol, drugs, and parties. He made a lot of money, but inside he felt empty. One day he decided to do something good, as well—something altruistic, something for the poor. His nightclubs were only open at night, and during the day he turned them into a kind of soup kitchen. Poor people could eat there for free and got some support. He went to the local church to facilitate this.

But after a year, his empty feeling wasn't gone. One day, Gareth spoke to one of the poor people he was welcoming during the day in his nightclubs. This guy told him that he should go to the church service on Sunday, which was held outside in a park. Gareth wasn't religious and didn't feel like it at first. But his hunger for something bigger that would give meaning to his life was greater than his aversion to religion. He went.

The church service and music began. Fifteen minutes in, he was already looking at his watch to see when it would be over. Gareth was annoyed and wanted to leave, but his wife, who was with him, was still watching, fascinated. So he stayed for a while. Suddenly, he had an experience where he saw Jesus and spoke to him. He was caught up in this vision and was so impressed by Jesus that he bumped into his wife and said, "I'm in love." His wife, who hadn't received this vision, got angry and said, "Who is it now, Gareth? That new chick you hired?" Gareth replied, "No, I'm in love with Jesus!" His wife became suspicious and asked if Gareth was on drugs. He said, "I'm completely sober, but I've met Jesus."

That meeting was the beginning of a new life for Gareth. He has sold all his nightclubs and casinos and now has all kinds of businesses in various countries. He is spending almost all the money that he doesn't need for his companies on charity work to help the poor and needy. His passion now is Jesus and making Jesus known. Living with Jesus gives him all he desires, which leads him to use his wealth for the benefit of others.

Significance of the Other

"It's not you who gives the world a place, but it's the Other[2] who speaks to you, who appeals to you, and who gives you a place," says philosopher Emmanuel Levinas. As human beings, we live in a network of relationships. These relationships determine our lives and our worth. Without relationships, we are nothing; we must realize that significance and meaning are given to us by the other. We alone cannot decide if we have meaning; our significance to the Other is up to the Other and not up to us. In the end, our meaningfulness is a gift to be received.

That's how I heard the story of Remco, a highly educated young professional. He had a job as a research assistant to the management of a large company. After giving three years of his life to this company, he wondered whether what he was doing had value for the business and the people he served. Would it matter if he didn't show up at work for one week? He put it to the test. He was absent for one week. What happened? Nobody had missed him, and nothing had gone wrong. This impacted Remco so deeply that he said farewell to business. His boss wanted to keep him, but his decision was made.

In search of himself and the meaning of life, Remco took a year off and went on a world trip. He discovered that life was not about systems, numbers, results, and market shares but about people. When he returned to his own country, he started a production company where he only employed hard-to-place people, people with a disadvantage in the labor market, and disabled people. He invested a lot of time and money in breaking down complex processes into simple routine tasks.

Remco selects his own employees and supports them personally. He talks to them often and tries to help them develop so that they can work somewhere else independently. Simple? Certainly not. He has often considered stopping. People turn out to be tricky, difficult, and sometimes ungrateful. Some don't arrive on time. Others suddenly, without giving a reason, do not come at all anymore. Others are depressed or aggressive. His business is a for-profit commercial company and must compete with others. Sometimes he finds himself pulling out his hair, trying to figure out how to survive or turn a situation around in a positive way.

Over time, Remco has begun to wonder why he gives his precious talent and time to these people. They put his profit, his performance, and his longevity at risk. Sometimes he feels like these people are bottomless pits: everything you put in them runs out just as fast. Luckily, there are also grateful people and positive exceptions. These rare successes keep him energized and on the move. These people give him meaning, joy, and gratefulness. His life and word count. When I asked Remco if he could hold on to this position and work even in the future because of the hardship and dissatisfaction, he replied: "I don't know. I don't know how long I can keep myself motivated to do this, but for now, I want to do it because I feel a calling in my life to do it and the rare moments of success are so rewarding that they keep me going."

The question remains: how can we connect our daily work to the larger picture of existence?

The Importance of Relationships

We are made for relationships. We are relational beings; this was part of our design.[3] It's through relationships that man arrives at his purpose. Friendships, romantic relationships, and all other relationships make up the fabric of life, giving it color. Biblical thinking about love and relationships as well-being is confirmed in a Harvard study. A study completed over a 75-year period[4] pointed to only one secret for happiness: loving relationships. The study examined relationships and communities in which you know yourself to be loved—in which you have been included, seen, and appreciated. "Close relationships, more than money or fame, are what keep people happy throughout their lives." Relationships keep us healthier and they make us happier. This shows us the importance of close relationships and stable marriages.

A nice story about stable relationships is Michael's story. One Friday evening after a long week of work, Dave invited Michael to have a drink and then to eat and go out. Dave, who was an entrepreneur, knew a place where lots of beautiful, wealthy, important men and women could be found—a place where one could quickly and easily have a "relationship" for a weekend. But Michael said, "You may think I'm boring, but I promised my wife that I would sit on the couch with her tonight, have a pizza together, and watch a movie." Then Dave suddenly got emotional and said, "Do you know why I'm going out to places like this? Because I hope to meet someone with whom I can sit on the couch to eat a pizza and watch a movie together."

Building stable family relationships is not always easy for an entrepreneur due to the long hours of work and the demands of the market. I talk with many of them about their family life, and what I have discovered is that sincere love is not so much connected to the amount of time you spend with your family, but rather how you behave at home when you are there.

For example, I think of Ian, a young entrepreneur who just started his company and is doing most of the work himself in this phase. He was asking me for advice in this area because his wife and children complained about his presence at home. I discovered that he needed the time at work but also that when he was at home, he wasn't really there. His mind was still at work. I advised him to be open to his wife and family and tell them that what they saw was true. He decided to pay attention to details of their lives and started to compliment them, ask about results at school, and talk about their friendships. He started to spend time with them, sitting with them on the couch and watching their television programs (although he would sometimes fall asleep during these moments). But his family saw that he was trying to do his best and that was enough. They saw that he loved them. That made the difference for them. Well-being in relationships is not about quantity but about quality.

Attitude is a choice.

Enjoying or being satisfied with our circumstances is also a choice and a critical part of our well-being. How we want to look at things is up to us. Our attitudes determine whether the glass is half full or half empty.

Dutch television host Otto de Bruijne, who had gone into a coma due to a medical mishap and as a result had to live with limitations, said:

> Do I want to live critical and angry because of the medical mistakes that happened to me? Do I want to live from out of all chaos and trouble that this caused me and that affects so many people in this world? Or do I want to see the life I lead as an answer? I want to be focused on God the giver; I want a responsive life. That's the choice. I want to live from gratitude. Yes, gratitude. From an active, proactive, even assertive gratitude. That gives freedom. That gives energy. That makes a person victorious: you don't have to fight against all of the negativity anymore.[5]

The final human freedom is the choice, under any circumstances, to determine one's own attitude and choose one's own path.

Happiness is a by-product.

Happiness for the Jerusalem person is derived from significance and meaning and is a by-product of one's surrender to another. For the Jerusalem entrepreneur, the meaning is found in living for another. It is found in a life that is bigger than himself. Love is the driving force. Paul writes in the Bible about love and significance. He says that what you do does not matter if it's not born of love. If you don't have love for others, your words and deeds are meaningless. They mean nothing. Even if you sell your property and give the money to the poor. Even if you die in a fire, fighting for a cause. None of these actions matter if they are done without love.[6]

Paul wants to inspire us with the example of Jesus, whose love for humanity was greater than his personal state of well-being. He writes, "Looking to Jesus, the founder and perfecter of our faith, who for the joy that was set before him endured the cross, despising the shame, and is seated at the right hand of the throne of God."[7] This kind of love gives joy and satisfaction and is valued by God our Father.

The Christian Jerusalem Entrepreneur

We have looked extensively and intensively at the Christian Jerusalem entrepreneur as a person. We did so because all doing comes from what we as people think, believe, and strive for in this world. We discovered that the Christian Jerusalem entrepreneur aims for the flourishing of man and creation. Love is his primary driver and living in connection is his reality check as he uses his talents and skills in worship to God. The way he is doing business is an expression of his faith. By living the art of entrepreneurship in this way, he is contributing to the well-being of individuals, society, and creation.

In the next part of this book, we are going to look at the characteristics of a Jerusalem company with God as the owner. We will discover why love in business is important, how you can build a resilient and long-lasting company, and what Jerusalem's earning models look like.

Section 3

A Jerusalem Company

11

Ownership

Before we start to talk about the Jerusalem company, it is important to understand ownership and our role as entrepreneurs within the company. In the Babylonian mindset, business is owned by an "earthly" owner, the shareholder, who can do whatever he wants with the business. Possessions and wealth are the great ideals of the Babylonian way of thinking. In Babylonian thinking, ownership is often a status symbol of power, success, and prestige. Nimrod kills and conquers to gain possessions. Babylon's great prostitute is desired for her property as well as her beauty. Many Christian entrepreneurs think in the same way and see their business as their own property.

Other Christian entrepreneurs may run their businesses with the concept of stewardship, but without God being involved. They want to be accountable to God for the choices they make yet tend to think from the perspective of business as private property. Martin is an example of this. Martin is a sincere Christian entrepreneur and likes to glorify God with his business, but in daily practice, he does not ask God for any advice about his business. He works very ethically, which means that he does not cheat, lie, or act badly toward others. Instead, he works with excellence, is generous, and uses his free time to be a responsible elder at the church.

He is successful in business and perceives this as God's blessing. Everyone speaks well about him because of his attitude and the way he works. But sometimes he hears Christian entrepreneurs talk with God about their business in a way that is foreign to him. They talk in such a way that it seems that God is the owner of their business. So he prayed to Jesus and asked him if there is something he lacked. It seemed to him that Jesus was saying: "Give me your business and follow me." It made him think, and now he is puzzled about the meaning of this.

What is God's perspective on ownership, and how should we view this? The general rule around Christian ownership is this: "The earth is the Lord's and the fullness thereof, the world and those who dwell therein."[1]

More specifically, the Bible speaks of the following components:

- The land: "The land shall not be sold in perpetuity, for the land is mine. For you are strangers and sojourners with me."[2]
- The animals: "For every beast of the forest is mine, the cattle on a thousand hills."[3]
- Gold and silver: "The silver is mine, and the gold is mine, declares the Lord of hosts."[4]
- Our bodies: "...for you were bought with a price. So glorify God in your body."[5]
- Our lives: "...who gave himself for us to redeem us from all lawlessness and to purify for himself a people for his own possession who are zealous for good works."[6]

Regarding ownership, Jesus says the following: "So therefore, any one of you who does not renounce all that he has cannot be my disciple."[7] So we can safely conclude that God owns everything here on earth.

Jesus also calls us to give our companies and our finances to him. We can see this when he spoke with the rich young man, known in the Bible as the rich young ruler, who in all respects obeyed God yet did not want to relinquish his possessions.

> And a rich young ruler asked him, "Good Teacher, what must I do to inherit eternal life?" And Jesus said to him, "Why do you call me good? No one is good except God alone. You know the commandments: Do not commit adultery, Do not murder, Do not steal, Do not bear false witness, Honor your father and mother." And he said, "All these I have kept from my youth." When Jesus heard this, he said to him, "One thing you still lack. Sell all that you have and distribute to the poor, and you will have treasure in heaven; and come, follow me." But when he heard these things, he became very sad, for he was extremely rich.[8]

Relinquishing our possessions and giving them to God is not easy, but it is fulfilling. It makes us free people. Imagine you are no longer imprisoned by the fear of losing your company or your possessions because you already gave them to God. Imagine that you can work hard, enjoy your work, and do it diligently, not because of profit, but because you are serving God and his goals. Imagine that you have access every morning to the wisest and most experienced counselor ever. One who knows your past, your future, your business, and where you are now. He is the one who controls everything in the end and will bring it to completion. Imagine having a business partner and boss like God. What would this be like? Relinquishment doesn't necessarily mean we have to sell everything and live in poverty, but it does mean that we must give up the mentality of our possessions as our personal property. God may use it in his own way.

This is also the conclusion Martin drew from his meeting with Jesus. He recognized himself as the rich young ruler and started a process to free himself from this idea of ownership.

Since then, Martin is on his journey of handing it over. He recognizes that it is easier to hand it over in your mind than practicing this in reality. But the process feels good to him. His biggest struggle is the resistance of his wife and his management team because they don't understand this process at all. Because of the radicality of the idea, he mostly keeps it for himself and doesn't want to manipulate people by saying, "God told me." He follows his own path and process.

I know entrepreneurs who have incorporated their large, attractive, flourishing businesses into a foundation and thus refrain from ownership and control. They have appointed a board of directors that advises on the strategy of the business and what to do with the funds. In prayer and mutual consultation, they try to understand God's voice. They are no longer the legal owner.

Others ask God for advice on their strategic choices, the sourcing policy of other businesses, locations, and sales policies. They try to understand God's voice because they see the business as being his. How does one deal with this ownership of God?

Ownership as an Idol

Material poverty is not God's vision for us because there is no honor to be found in poverty. It makes people dependent and can drive them to dishonesty and theft. However, it is important to free ourselves from the idea that we own something. What we call personal property belongs to God. Ownership of earthly possessions is a responsibility. We came to this earth with nothing, and we will leave with nothing. The earth and our lives have been given to us, not as personal property but on loan to love and serve others.

If we don't separate ourselves from our possessions and wealth and renounce them as being our own, they will work against us negatively, becoming an idol and imprisoning us. Some people, therefore, become greedy, while others become anxious because they are afraid of losing their acquired possessions.

In 2008 and 2009, at the start of the financial crisis, I met entrepreneurs who had completely lost their way. I talked to people who wanted to remove their money from the banks and invest it in real estate and gold because they didn't trust the banking system anymore. One person wanted to convert his assets into gold to keep at home. There was even someone who, no longer able to cope with life because of financial losses, committed suicide.

An entrepreneur with more than a few generous assets complained that his wife thought she no longer could spend money because they had lost half of their assets. She was struck with blind fear and panic with millions still at her fingertips. They were all bound to their possessions as security and identity. They were not free and expected their well-being to come from their money and possessions instead of God.

Some people have high expectations of what wealth and possessions will give them but don't see their expectations met. They seek happiness and well-being in their money and property but do not find it. Some are lonely because they no longer trust anyone. They hire guards and drive around in armored cars. Others die just as they decide they want to enjoy themselves. Whether someone can enjoy his wealth is not determined by what he owns, but by God. As the writer of Ecclesiastes says, "The ability to enjoy your wealth and possessions is a gift from God."[9]

Our Problem of Wealth

With respect to our possessions, the biggest problem in the wealthiest countries is not poverty, but our wealth. We often do not know how to deal with our affluence, so we are creating an artificial world with our resources in which we exclude others. Take San Francisco, which for years has been a city of extremes.

Because of the wealth brought by the tech industry, an income of less than $117,400 a year for a family of four is now regarded as low. A two-bedroom house costs $1.3 million.

Yet this wealth has another side. As a San Franciscan, if you don't earn more than $100,000 every year, you can't keep up. In a city with 885,000 inhabitants, 4,400 people sleep on the streets every night. The city has been trying to do something about the enormous number of homeless for years, but some of the richest people do not cooperate. As Mayor London Breed told *The San Francisco Chronicle,* "People want us to help our homeless people find housing, but it's incredibly frustrating and disappointing that as soon as we propose a plan for shelters, people threaten to take legal action."

Wealth can create arrogance and a lack of compassion. This was the same for Jim, who told me his story after he had come to faith in Jesus. In his old life, he didn't care about people. Jim said, "I never thought about how badly people would feel about business decisions. Feelings were for the weak souls and soft hearts of ordinary people. I was king in my world of business and money. I lived in my bubble of boardrooms, private jets, parties, nice ladies, and money. I thought that everything in life came down to choosing and that everyone could become like me if they wanted to. My wealth and way of life blinded me. I was hard on people. I humiliated and fired people when I felt bad about myself just to blame someone. I was not thinking of the personal consequences for them. I comforted myself with the thought that they were able to have the same life I had but didn't deserve it because they made poor choices."

Another story of living in your wealth bubble and losing the connection to reality is the one of the well-to-do fathers who took his son on a sort of educational vacation to show him how poor some people are. They stayed a few days on the farm of a poor family. On the way back, the father asked the son, "What have you learned from this holiday?" The son answered, "We only have one dog, they have four. We have a swimming pool; they have a large lake nearby. We light the lamps at night, they have the stars. We always buy our food, but their food grows on the land. We have a home movie theater to watch nature movies, but they live in nature. We have a large fence and cameras to protect us, they have friends. Thank you, Dad, for showing me how poor we are."[10]

How can we turn wealth into a blessing without losing perspective?

Prosperity as a Blessing

Some Christians say we have to live in poverty—that prosperity and wealth are earthly pleasures we must deny ourselves. Some Christians also say we should not be rich because we have to give everything away, that faith coincides with a minimalist lifestyle. No wealth, no prosperity, no abundance.

But in the Old Testament, prosperity and abundance are always seen as a blessing.[11] The promised land, Canaan, is flowing with milk and honey and is a land of abundance.[12] God even said:

> You shall remember the Lord your God, for it is he who gives you the power to get wealth, that he may confirm his covenant that he swore to your fathers, as it is this day. And if you forget the Lord your God and go after other gods and serve them and worship them, I solemnly warn you today that you shall surely perish.[13]

God is the one who wants you to prosper.[14] The New Jerusalem and the new earth are characterized by abundance and the absence of lack.[15] Beauty and wealth are not foul concepts, but noble goals that we can pursue. Nor is there any government praised for keeping its population impoverished.

Poverty in itself is not a Christian aspiration, although it can serve a purpose. The question is not whether we should be rich or poor, but what we have done with what we have received.

In the parable of the talents, we see that God gives something to everyone.[16] This is not about the amount that everyone gets because that is different for everyone. In this parable, the point is what we have done with what we have received. Did we handle it responsibly and act in the interest of the owner? In the end, we are all equally rich and poor, because all we have is from God as the rightful owner. We are only stewards, and the command is to multiply and increase so that we can bless others.

Paul says that we may enjoy what has been given to us in addition to spreading the blessing of our wealth. As he writes to Timothy in 1 Timothy 6:17-19:

> As for the rich in this present age, charge them not to be haughty, nor to set their hopes on the uncertainty of riches, but on God, who richly provides us with everything to enjoy.

It is challenging to balance being a blessing and enjoying your wealth at the same time. You can only solve this by making generosity one of your desires and the fulfillment of your heart. The key to unlocking this challenge is love. If we start to love people, we are eager to love and serve them with all our resources, including our finances. Take Ruben for instance. Ruben was a wealthy entrepreneur, but his wealth didn't give him any satisfaction. He was afraid of losing it because it was his security. Nowadays, he is very generous on all levels of his life and told me: "When God put his love in my heart, I started to change and found fulfillment in helping people. Not that I am holy and generous at all times, because sometimes someone is calling me and I start praying to God that they will not ask for money."

When I asked him how he made decisions about granting people their requests for money, he said: "I always ask God first.

I ask God if giving money is the best thing I can do to serve them with their request. Several times God told me not to give, but to give them advice about their work or personal life. Then I am generous with my knowledge and expertise. I also discovered that some don't care about my opinion or what God has to tell them, they just want the money."

Letting Go and Becoming Free

As disciples of Jesus, we want to give everything to him, but many of us know that we don't always do this. Even in what we call total surrender, we are often still imperfect and "works in progress." In Jesus's time, this imperfect devotion raised the following question: "Those who heard it said, 'Then who can be saved?' But he said, 'What is impossible with man is possible with God.'"[17] Fortunately, our salvation depends on God and we live by His grace. So the choice of who we want to be in this day and age is not about our salvation but about our desire.

The choice of following Jesus and total surrender is a choice with positive consequences.

> And [Jesus] said to them, "Truly, I say to you, there is no one who has left house or wife or brothers or parents or children, for the sake of the kingdom of God, who will not receive many times more in this time, and in the age to come eternal life."[18]

In letting go of our possessions and our material wealth, God gives us everything we need—and more. God responds to our dedication to the fulfillment of the desires of our hearts. Often, we don't know about these until we have received his fulfillment, as we discovered in the stories of Jim and Ruben. They received compassion and love, which was new to them. Now they are extremely happy with it. It changed their behavior and life.

What God wants to give us is an extension of God's vision for humanity, namely that we become human beings in the image and likeness of Christ. The reward is that we experience God's love and presence, which gives inner peace and transcends all other human desires we can have. Therefore, we need to be freed from our possessions. This freedom from ownership is a blessing, as the many stories in this chapter show. It is hard and difficult, but unbelievably rewarding.

12

Decision-Making

God, the ultimate owner, wants to share his riches, possessions, and splendor with us. We, as followers of Jesus, would like to serve God and share our lives with God and Jesus. It is this unity of God and man in which our salvation and well-being lie. It's not about renouncing ownership but about a personal surrender to Jesus. Jesus asks us as entrepreneurs, "Will you give your life and your company to me so that business can function to honor God and to bless people?" Saying yes makes us disciples in the marketplace and business and gives us a unique role as Christian entrepreneurs.

Whereas stewardship is usually about recognizing God as the true owner and applying God's rules and principles to business, discipleship goes a step further. Discipleship is about surrender, listening to the voice of God in specific situations, being led by his Spirit, and handing over the authority over our lives and business to Jesus. They speak, make decisions, and are in control, and I follow.

Strategy

Owned by God, the corporate strategy becomes a spiritual business, a form of discipleship. The purposes of our company and our investments are not to solely increase our financial capital. This may be a method to achieve other goals, but the goal of our company is determined by what God wants with it. How and where does God want His money and business to bear fruit, and in what way?

I know entrepreneurs, for example, who have a good company in the Netherlands and consciously choose not to maximize profits. They prefer to invest in businesses in poor countries and regions to provide people with work and income there. And I know entrepreneurs who choose to work with disabled and underprivileged people in their company or who only want to work sustainably or biologically. In their strategy and their choices, they have been guided by the understanding of God's voice for their lives and businesses.

God's voice is not only one from the past but is a voice that wants to speak in our lives in the here and now. He wants to talk about our companies and our daily lives. They are both his. It is striking how Jesus, who has already arrived in heaven, speaks to Paul when Paul is persecuting Jesus' disciples. He does not ask Paul why he persecutes his disciples, but why Paul persecutes *him*, Jesus.[1] Jesus deeply identifies with his disciples.

My prayer has changed from "Lord, will you bless this day and my work?" to "Lord, what do you want me to do with your company today?" And "How do you want us to solve the cash flow problem?" or "How do you want the conflict with our supplier resolved?

There are already many entrepreneurs who start the day this way, listening for the voice of God before going to work. There are management teams who spend Monday morning with God, praying for the week ahead. Some salespeople pray before meetings with clients. God and Jesus want to be actively involved in our lives and businesses because it is also their lives and their businesses. In this role, one of our most important actions of Christian entrepreneurship is listening.

Listen First

Listening is not the same as hearing. Hearing is lending an ear to what has been said but does not necessarily lead to action. Listening is understanding the other person's nature and intentions and then responding to the other person's context. Our reactions and follow-up actions indicate how well we have listened.

Listening and involving God in our lives is one of the most important challenges and tasks we have as Christians. Jesus' earthly life was focused on listening to God. "Man shall not live by bread alone, but by every word that comes from the mouth of God."[2] We read often in the Bible that Jesus went to pray before making decisions.[3] Prayer and alignment with God were his practice,[4] and Jesus took the time for this, even when he was busy. "

Too Busy Not to Pray

Sometimes our business is the reason we cannot pray or don't spend time with God. But it's just when we're experiencing pressure and tension that we need time to be still and to reflect with God about our lives. New insights, ideas, and out of the box thinking require time, reflection, and inspiration. God wants to give all of this as we seek him in our busyness. Not only does he want to speak in our lives,[5] but he wants to be sought[6] and asked.[7]

Listening requires practice.

Really hearing what's being said isn't easy. We know this from our business experiences and daily lives. How many conflicts and mistakes in our businesses are the results of poor communication even though we do talk to each other? Too often, our prejudices and our own thoughts determine what we believe we are hearing. We can speak the same words, but due to a different context, education, culture, or life choice, the words have a different meaning.

Before we can listen to the other person properly, we must get to know and understand the other person. This requires time, practice, and shared experiences. That is why, just like Jesus, it is good to tune into God on a daily basis in our work and keep an open connection with him throughout the day. By making a habit of this, we learn to understand God's voice.

Time with God

How can you practice this listening? What can spending time with God for work look like? My personal time with God is as follows. On a normal day, I get up at 6 a.m. I shower, prepare my breakfast, scan the newspaper, and then meet with God. In this time, I first evaluate the previous day, writing down what I have experienced. I see if there are any action points or loose ends I have to deal with. I thank God and pray for people I have met, asking God to be with me. Then I look at the day to come in my schedule. I pray for the day and for the meetings I will have. At the same time, I outline the day ahead.

Then I read from the Bible or a devotional. I alternate this regularly to change up the day's rhythm. When I read my Bible, I'm not just seeking knowledge or information—I'm desiring to meet God. For this reason, I use the Lectio Divina method. This means that as I'm reading the day's text, I want my thoughts to be quiet and peaceful so that the Holy Spirit can speak into my life. Then I read the text once in its entirety. I read the text again and underline the words that speak to me. I reflect on these words or phrases. Why do those words stand out? What do they have to say to me? How do they affect my life? Finally, I read the text once more.

After that, I finish by praying through the text. That is, I thank God for his message, I pray about where the text speaks to me, where my responsibilities are, and where the text touches our world and environment. Finally, I pray for the people on my prayer list. Then I go to work. The time with God usually lasts 30 minutes. The total morning ritual, including newspaper, breakfast, and showering, takes about an hour and a half. Between half-past seven and eight, I go to work.

If this seems very structured, it is. It suits me. Every person develops, if all is well, a habit that suits his or her personality and language of faith. The form and structure are not important, but the search for the daily connection with God is.

The beauty of God is that he speaks to everyone in their own language.[8] One hears God's voice in the silence, another in a dream or vision. Another understands God through the words of other people. Some by investigating the circumstances with their insight and minds, and still others by reading the Bible. Most of us use multiple languages to understand God. How we understand God is not so important, but the fact that we want to seek him is.[9] God wants to be wanted. Of course, there are days and periods where the "normal" rhythms cannot take place. Circumstances can cause you to change your daily rhythm, but having this habit of tuning in with God on a daily basis is very beneficial.

God wants to be involved in our life as an entrepreneur, friend, father/mother, and partner. We can go to God for advice;[10] he longs for this intimacy.[11] This "quiet" time and our prayers are not always about seeking advice or achieving an intended result. God is not a source of information to be used so that we can benefit our own lives. At its deepest, time with God is about intimacy, like a love affair.[12] We love God for who he is and not for what he gives. This is important to remember.

Living in Freedom

You might be thinking that if God wants to speak in every situation, then there is no longer freedom to act as we want. That is not the case. God does want to be on the journey with us, but he does not want to determine and define everything for us. After all, we are not puppets: we are created in God's image.[13] We may freely make choices, be creative, dream, and choose our life's passion.

Our daily contact with God is a bit like a parent-child relationship. Everyone has his own life, and the adult child makes his own choices. Yet he still enjoys being together with the parent (and vice versa). They talk about life; sometimes the parent gives advice and sometimes not. Sometimes the parent finds it more important that his or her child makes their own discoveries. Sometimes the parent wants to share his or her opinions or thoughts on what the child finds important. Sharing life is important, but character growth and maturing into adulthood are sometimes more important than giving the right advice at the right time. This is the way God is with us in our relationship with him.

God the Father sometimes advises us because some themes are very important. But it may be that God wants to know what is going on in our hearts and, therefore, remains silent or allows us to go down a difficult path.[14] Sometimes God does not want to lead our business into success or offer us the shortest and easiest way but, rather, wants to shape us.[15]

God will accomplish His purposes.

The guiding principles that God offers us by giving us free will are clear and concise. The prophet Micah says, "He has told you, O man, what is good; and what does the Lord require of you but to do justice, and to love kindness, and to walk humbly with your God?"[16]

Jesus summarizes God's life-giving words as follows: "You shall love the Lord your God with all your heart and with all your soul and with all your mind. This is the great and first commandment."[17] This is our mission. You could say that we as humans have a role in accomplishing God's will.

Of course, there is also a divine side. The divine side of God's will is that "what God wants will come to pass." God always achieves his purposes; we don't have to worry about that.[18] God achieves his plans in his own sovereign way through our good and bad choices. This is the grace of God. We can marry, build buildings, start businesses, and make decisions according to our hearts and desires, all within his advice and precepts. We can trust that God will lead us to life-giving fullness.[19] The point of our listening is not so that we may achieve our purposes, but that God may achieve his purposes in us.

Learning from Our Decisions

We should know that, in living with God, there are actually no bad decisions. God can use everything for growth and for good. What's important is the heart, not the outcome. Of course, the fact is that decisions have consequences. Some decisions have very painful repercussions, but we can learn from each decision and its consequences. Failing is not making the wrong decision; failing is refusing to learn and continuing to make wrong decisions. We can always begin again. Every decision teaches us something about ourselves, about God, and about our current situation. So there are no wrong decisions in this sense. The point is what we do with the outcome of our decisions. Do the next steps lead to growth and life or do they lead to misery and death?

The liberating thing about God's involvement is that he wants to be present in all of our decisions. He is able to build something good, even out of our wrong intentions or poorly executed decisions.[20] Of course, we want to make our decisions very carefully because any painful consequences can also affect others who may have had no influence on the decision but bear the consequences.

Making (Business) Decisions

Before making a business decision, it is important to consult with all stakeholders (as far as possible). God's voice is also part of this process because he is one of the stakeholders. Our decisions should be made to serve people and allow them to flourish.

A handy way to test our choices and decisions for our businesses is the so-called five beacons tool. This tool gives five points of reference which function independently of each other. In our test, we examine whether the five reference points speak the same language and send out the same signal. If one or more of the reference points sends out a different signal, this is a reason to stop and further investigate our decision. You can see it as a kind of evaluation tool, a test to examine the decisions you want to make and ensure that the decisions are wise and in line with God's ways.

The five points of reference are:

- *Prayer*. When I think about a decision, what comes to mind in my quiet time and what understanding does that give me? Do I experience these as God's thoughts, and do I have peace about them?
- *The Bible.* Is what I want to do aligned with God's Word? What wisdom and guidelines does the Bible have in this situation? Are there examples and similar situations in the Bible that point in a direction?
- *Circumstances*. What is happening in my life, business, and in the world? How do I understand the events that take place in my life?
- *Counselors and advisors.* What are they telling me? Do I allow people in my environment who dare to contradict me? What does my husband or wife

tell me? He/she is often 50% of God's wisdom in my life. Do I choose a board of directors and/or supervisory directors whom I hold in high esteem, but who are independent and also speak out against me if it's needed? Do I have an accountability group of like-minded people and wise friends? Do I have a good mentor or coach, and am I a good mentor or coach for others?

- *The rational mind.* God has given us reasoning capabilities. When I consider the situation, is it logical?

The evaluation of these points may, of course, include a degree of subjectivity and wishful thinking, but if all five give the same results, then usually we can proceed calmly. These five points are a good test if the decisions I want to make are in line with what God wants from me as an entrepreneur.

However, sometimes you might not get them aligned and you feel tension. In that case, after taking some time to consider and speak with wise counselors, we must decide anyway. What do you do then? My advice is not to be afraid and not to become passive. Sometimes God only speaks when we have already begun the journey. The rudder of a ship only works when the ship sails. Sometimes God can only speak when we are already on our way. Still, there are situations where you don't have the tangible confirmation of God speaking to you. It continues to be important to move and act from a sense of peace, knowing that God's favor rests on you and that his grace and love is bigger than your actions.

Bear Consequences

For healthy business decisions, it is important that the decision-maker is involved and bears the consequences of his own decision. In this way, decisions will be taken more carefully.

There is no one-size-fits-all.

How we understand God and *how* that shapes our business has a lot to do with our backgrounds, cultures, experiences, and preferences. We also have our basic values as well as the implementation of these values. The implementation of faith in our day-to-day activities has a lot to do with our faith language. Some entrepreneurs work within a circular economy, attaching great value to sustainability, while other entrepreneurs consider human rights policies and the development of employees as very important.

A third type of entrepreneur attaches great importance to the significance of technological progress to make the world a better place. Still others find the right words to speak about what God has done for them personally. All these business people distinguish themselves in their own way, finding their inspiration in the same faith and values. God speaks in his own way to each of them, as each one contributes their unique gifting.

A good example of someone who understood God in a special way and started to do business in a unique way is Christine, who manufactures plastic products. Christine is a leader in her field with several factories on different continents. God speaks to her in different ways. How God speaks determines her business trajectory. For example, she developed a model based upon the growth created by the right conditions and the right basic principles and ensured that the management of the company was based on making space for growth opportunities instead of targets and action plans. Christine's process is outlined below.

1. On one of her travels to Indonesia, she passed by a garbage dump, where she saw her products among the waste. The problem of pollution was so close to her heart that at that moment, she decided to work within a fully circular recycled model with full reuse of her products.
2. She discovered a growth model based on biotic principles[21] that derived its values from the growth of living organisms and plants. The idea behind this is that growth takes place if we create the right circumstances, as you can see in nature. She believes we should provide the right environment and minimize obstacles to ensure natural development. She decided to apply these natural principles within her company. She started to move from organizational thinking, which is about controlling processes, to a lean natural structure that creates its own processes and growth. She understood the value of having a network of specialists that were not part of her own business. She called this network surrounding her company an ecosystem. She saw the principle of symbiosis and the coexistence of different species that are mutually beneficial to each other as a template for the interaction between the various fields, types of people, and businesses. In developing this and making it bear fruit, she granted a lot of freedom to the various disciplines within the company and in the collaboration with others. Like in creation and biology, all the separate components—from the small microorganism to the gigantic stars—are interconnected and regulate each other. The way all parts work together was more important to her than

the individual parts themselves. This interaction between disciplines, fields of expertise, and personal freedom to contribute to the whole lead to diversity, innovation, and healthy business practices.

3. Under her leadership, protecting a business philosophy based upon identity and principles was a priority, and she concerned herself with implementing and multiplying these values and principles in people. If her people were able to work according to certain principles and values, they could solve problems themselves and would need less management supervision. She was convinced that this was the way to foster responsible and mature employees.
4. She was led by God's voice as she met with people and as she grew in her personal understanding of God's voice.

A completely different illustration of how entrepreneurs are used uniquely by God is the example of Martin, an entrepreneur active in the food industry. Martin found himself doing well, and he was looking for the next challenge. Did he need to expand his business or do something else within the food industry? He didn't know the answer and decided to pray about it.

He got the feeling that he was supposed to go to another country and set up a software company there. But his knowledge of software was limited, and he admittedly didn't know much about the country where he was thinking of doing business. Martin decided to fly to this country anyway to see what would happen. There he met people from the software industry who were looking for an investor. He saw this as a confirmation and decided to set up a software company with them. Over time, he accumulated more business and the company grew. With his new partners, who turned out to be Christians, he decided to use his profits to print Bibles for that country. Now this country is spiritually nourished by the proceeds of his company. Martin feels like a blessed man and feels affirmed by what came from the first steps he took in faith.

I also know an entrepreneur, Victor, who in his quiet time received a message from God that he should take some time off from his company. In faith, he decided to hand over the daily management to his management team and prepared the team for an undetermined period when he wouldn't be active. A month after he did this, Victor received a visit from his pastor. The pastor asked Victor if he would consider taking over the leadership of the church for a year because he wanted to go on a sabbatical. Victor asked his pastor why he came to him. The preacher answered, "I told God in my quiet time that I was ready for a sabbatical, but I couldn't imagine being able to take it. Who would take over the duties of the church? Then your name came to mind. It took me a month to discern if this is really from God. I think it is, which is why I'm here. But I don't know if this is realistic, because you have a big company that depends on you."

Victor laughed heartily and told the pastor that God told him a month ago to take a step back from the operational part of his company and that he'd already taken the steps to do so. Six months later, Victor-the-entrepreneur became Victor-the-pastor for one year. He learned a lot about leadership and how people are connected to a culture, and what it takes to change a culture. Victor is back in business and working in his own company again, where he now understands that culture means everything. He now desires to work toward a healthy Christian business culture in his company.

There is also the story of Jake, a young Christian entrepreneur who was extremely successful in his early years. God spoke to him through his marriage, and that changed him as a person. Successful and charismatic, Jake was loved and respected by his staff and by his shareholders. New businesses were begun, and all these businesses flourished with his successful approaches and strategies. But his attitude slowly changed from serving clients and employees to using clients and employees for his personal ambitions and professional success. The continued appreciation for his work successes meant that his ego continued to grow.

Everything seemed wonderful until one night he came home and his wife told him she wanted a divorce. His world collapsed. He was completely blindsided. He was successful, had a good income, gave away money, went to church every week, and was there for people when they needed him.

When he told her that he didn't understand, his wife replied, "This is exactly the problem. You're all wrapped up in your own perspective, but are you still able to get out of yourself and imagine what other people are feeling or experiencing? Do you still value people for their intrinsic value of just being human beings?"

He was bewildered. "What do you mean?" he asked.

She said, "You used to love me and the children for who we were, but now it feels like you only love us if we can mean something to you. All you seem to care about is having a fun time, that we are this pleasant family, and a non-needy outlet for all of your feelings and emotions, good and bad. As long as you get enough attention, you are happy, but what about us? Do you ever think about our importance, our lives, and who *we* are?"

This was a revelation to Jake. He immediately realized that his wife was right—he had become self-centered, only thinking about his own ambitions and from his perspective. He had recently fired an older employee who had only a few years before he retired. He had used a business incident to dispose of this man as an expensive cost item. And last month he had fired a production manager because his salary was quite high, yet he was not very liked by the other employees, had burnout, and was no longer able to work the way he had before the burnout. Jake was a Christian and gave away a lot of money, but if he was honest, it was mostly about his own prestige within the church. He was not involved in the church at a personal level; he gave because he was asked to give.

Jake decided to change. He wanted to dedicate himself to God again and do it God's way. He wanted the Holy Spirit to change him into a better man. And along the way, Jake did change. His close family and friends noticed that he had become more attentive. Details became more important, contradictions were acknowledged, and somehow, he was becoming a new man.

His management team found him to be a softer version of the old Jake. The profit figures remained the same but had become less important. Jake experienced more satisfaction in his work, and the atmosphere at work had changed for the better. He understood that it was God speaking through his wife's criticism and it was God who was with him in the following time of reflection. Jake's experience changed his family life and way of doing business—for good.

These are just ordinary stories of ordinary entrepreneurs with a desire to understand God's voice. The consequence was that it changed and impacted their lives and businesses for good.

13

Love in Business

Is it even possible for us as entrepreneurs to work in love within a highly competitive environment? Is it possible to run a business where love is the foundation in a Babylonian culture? Can love function as one of the alternative strategies, making us as Jerusalem entrepreneurs wiser and more impactful than our colleagues from Babylon?

Let me introduce you to Daniel—a tough, straight forward entrepreneur. He is fair and honest and shows his love for people by helping them grow and become mature. Daniel represents what I call masculine love. Masculine love distinguishes itself from feminine love in that it focuses on making people mature, independent, well-educated, and resilient. In that way, they can care for their own life and future because they learned it.

The driver for Daniel's behavior is love; he has the best in mind for others by helping them become healthy, mature individuals who can take care of themselves and their families. Masculine love is different from what I call feminine love, which is focused on caring, avoiding pain and troubles, and keeping people close so no harm will be done to them. Feminine love has a tendency to protect and take over responsibilities when times get tough. These two kinds of love are important and need to be balanced, as the story of Daniel will show. Daniel was not always guided by a balanced sense of love. He had had a tough upbringing. The message was: "be tough and hard and control your life; otherwise, others will control you." When he made mistakes in his youth, he got beaten. The beating was explained as being educational, a tool to help him to improve. Daniel was hurt by this beating. It did not come from a place of love but from a place of rage and anger. His father, however, explained it as tough love, which confused Daniel. This so-called love started to shape Daniel's thinking and actions toward others. For a long time, Daniel practiced this kind of behavior himself.

When Daniel came to Christ, his heart started to change. He started to feel awful about himself and his behavior. He understood that he had to love people, but he didn't know how to do this. Did he have to express his love in the same way he did toward his mother and sisters, being caring and protecting? How would that kind of love work in making difficult business decisions or negotiations with distributors?

His confusion grew so much that he thought that love and business could not go together. But then there was a point of change. He went on a trip to the desert with other entrepreneurs to discover more about God and about himself. He talked with one of the female participants about his problem. This lady helped him understand the two kinds of love. She explained to him that maturing other people and helping them grow can also be an act of love when you do it from the perspective of sincerely helping them.

Daniel escaped his confusion by seeing that these two kinds of love needed to be balanced or they would harm people. Just giving penalties to improve behavior without a touch of feminine, empathic love, which takes into account the others' weaknesses, would be harsh and would reflect his past behavior. At the same time, only caring without helping people become mature can make them weak and dependent. The challenge in business is to balance these two kinds of love.

Love is a characteristic of the Jerusalem entrepreneur. Because the word *love* is often wrongly understood and used in various ways, it's a good idea to first define what I mean when I use it. I use the word love in the context of two Greek terms for love,[1] *philia* and *agape*. *Philia* means a mutual love between friends and relatives, while *agape* refers to a love for the person in his entirety. This implies that this love should contribute to the well-being of the person, without negative feelings about the person or our opponent. This kind of love comes from an inner source, something in us that wants to share itself.

Agape is able to love the other, the self,[2] and the world around us without condition. It is a love that gives without expecting anything in return, a love that wants everyone and everything to thrive. *Agape* is the central theme beyond all principles and laws God has given to man.[3] He desires that this love will determine our behavior and actions. The word love in this chapter centers around these two types, *philia* and *agape*, and not *eros*, romantic love.

This chapter is about creating a culture where love can flourish. I will discuss love in employee relationships, love in customer relationships, and love in supplier relationships.

The boardroom determines the culture.

When visiting a company, one can quickly estimate something of its management style and business culture. Sometimes when walking with a manager through the office space to his office, I've noticed that the buzz of the employees suddenly becomes silent. Computer screens are flickering, and everyone is seemingly hard at work, yet as soon as I leave, the screens flicker again, people stand up, and the office murmur returns. This behavior is usually a symptom of a fear culture, often caused by a dominant leadership style where there is little love or grace.

In other companies, I notice an open atmosphere where people talk to each other. The computer screens don't flicker because they are changing the program they are working in. When their manager passes by, employees joke around with him respectfully. This is a culture of appreciation and respect with a focus on people. This open culture is determined by its supervisors and management team.

The conversations in the boardroom determine the business culture. The way management and supervisors speak determines the culture of the company. Sometimes I hear managers talking derogatively about others. Women are objectified or employees are considered losers. Some see their employees as instruments and production machines, while others talk about them in terms of costs. If we no longer call people by their names, they lose value. When we no longer deal with our employees, customers, and suppliers as individuals, dehumanization occurs. When we think of people as potential, good ideas, or investments, people become objectified. We will continue to look at people as instruments for our own use.

I have heard how deeply people who thought they were valuable and special to their company or employers have been hurt because, along the way, they discovered that they were only seen as an employee, an instrument, or a cost. I have seen and experienced company cultures that demonized and harassed their people. I have also seen too much of so-called company loyalty at the expense of the employees, or how managers have become part of a group culture without the courage to be themselves or to resist a group culture that excluded people and treated others inferiorly. The desire to be appreciated, the peer pressure, the culture, the success, and the prestige were all stronger than one's own identity and the will to live from one's own values and convictions.

These types of businesses sometimes resemble a jungle in which only the fittest can survive. There are even businesses that lay off 1–2% of their staff every year as standard practice to retain the best and to get new, better people. However, business doesn't have to be this cutthroat. While love in the business world is by no means a given, it can be done.

How do you create a different business culture?

Creating a culture of love in business takes intentional action. Personal attention, genuine interest, and personal involvement with people are all important, but so is being straight and just. Jerusalem love tries to help the person become the person God designed him or her to be. For example, I know a company where the managers have weekly private conversations with their immediate staff. For this reason, their "span of control" is limited to five or six people. A characteristic of this conversation is that it is not about the business side but about personal matters. Their starting point in leadership is, "Know your employees, let them grow, and show them your love." Their credo for managers regarding employees is, "They are your mission; their work is their mission." This personal care for people is central and stems from a desire to help develop people and let them grow in their God-given potential. Of course, this only works if there is sincere love, mutual influence, safety, and openness.

Real love in business requires a change of culture, an adjustment in attitude, and different behavior. Many of today's managers may need further training or may need to learn to love themselves first before they can love others, but love can be learned.

I know a very task-oriented manager who thinks in terms of goals and tasks but has now made love his goal and focus. He changed because he saw the impact of love in the company by the way the owner-operated people wanted to be connected to the owner and his way of behavior. He started to learn how to love by watching his boss and just practicing his behavior. It's great to see how people react to his sincere but somewhat clumsy attempts to work in a more people-oriented way. He is respected because the employees see that although interest in others does not come naturally to him, he tries his best. His people now do anything for him.

A good friend, Stefan, who has a large, wonderful company, once shared his vision on entrepreneurship with fellow entrepreneurs. God's love is one of his motivations, and he tries to convey it within his company's culture. Stefan is passionate about telling stories, and the room got quiet as he said, "All my employees know that they are loved." Several entrepreneurs had tears in their eyes as he said this. This is another place where we can see that we are all people who need love. Love makes all the difference. We are not loved for what we do, but who we are.

From my experience, it is a challenge for many executives to steep their business in an understanding of love and loving relationships. Healthy relationships and being connected to each other in love transform the culture of a business and make businesses more competitive in every respect. If, however, becoming more competitive has become the motive for love, then real love has already been lost. Love is fragile and vulnerable and only works if it is authentic and true.

You have to be the change you want to see.

Within the business, we cannot outsource love to the human resources managers or external coaches. We, as managers, must be the change that we aim for. We must practice and be love ourselves; otherwise, it won't work. It must be an intrinsic part of our leadership and management.

I know an entrepreneur named Randy who wanted his company to be known for its service. He felt that he was not the symbol of this change he wanted to see. He was not very friendly and service-minded. He wanted to be service-minded because he believed it could make him the number one company in his field. As a manager, he was no longer active in the direct operation of a business but lived in the comfort zone of success and attention, leading his business by inspiring and advising. He tried to steer the improvement of customer service from above, without being involved himself, but with the focus on specific details and people's attitudes. Randy started writing guidelines, influencing middle management, and training people. However, this did not produce the results he desired.

Randy then went on to look for a good coach, a change agent to help shape this process within his company. After going through all of the potentials with their beautiful stories and quotes, he met a senior manager with whom he immediately clicked. This guy had both a lot of experience and a lot of wisdom. Randy believed he was the right man to give shape to this process.

After an introductory meeting, the advisor soon realized where the mistake was and he said to Randy, "If you don't change yourself and become the change agent of your desired culture, nothing will change. Otherwise, there's nothing I can do to help you." Randy realized that the consultant was right but did not want to change his behavior. And so everything remained as it was.

Cultural changes start at the top with the owners and presidents.

Investing in Change

The value of the person within a company is determined by the heart of the management team. When a management team has love as its motivation, it will focus on employee growth and success. Making people work to their strengths is the challenge. The better their personalities, motivating circumstances, talents, and values fit their work, the higher the motivation, quality of the work, and employee satisfaction.

Putting the right people in the right place begins with careful vetting. We as managers look not only at talent and education but also at personality, character, values, and whether someone clicks with the team. We focus on the three C's: Competence, Character, and Click. It's better to keep a vacancy open than to add someone to the team who doesn't fit. The general advice? When in doubt, don't hire.

Over time, some employees may no longer fit within the organization. This could be due to changing work circumstances, job performance, the times, or the culture. For example, a car mechanic has quickly gone from a mechanical repairman to a service-oriented ICT and electronics specialist. A carpenter must now be able to operate and maintain a fully digital lathe with equipment. This means that existing employees need to participate in and receive further training. It means training people within the business or, if they cannot be developed to another level, guiding them to a workplace outside the business.

Letting them stay out of loyalty is not love. Slowly, the employee will become dissatisfied and the rest of the organization will become frustrated. Moreover, we deprive talented people of the opportunity to use their qualities if we always allow existing employees to retain their positions. How do we deal well with employees who are no longer a good fit for the organization?

Of course, these problems don't appear out of thin air; they are often the results of a long and slow process. How do you, as a manager, keep a sharp eye on what problems are growing and prevent them? The key to keeping people enlightened about their progress is regular and thorough performance interviews. These interviews are additionally important for us as managers to get a sense of where our employees are. Depending on the situation and circumstances, we can work on retraining, continued training, or the joint search for a different workplace. This conversation with the employee in which he becomes vulnerable with all of his qualities, talents, and weaknesses is important. These conversations allow us to express our expectation as well. This dialogue is key to understanding each other based on love. Only in mutual communication can we find solutions together.

An Exit Strategy

Sometimes reassessing an employee's strengths, weaknesses, and work performance leads to an exit strategy. If employees are no longer able to function within the company, it may be in their interest to leave. A good and healthy workplace is the priority, especially when people are dealing with all kinds of tensions and no longer experiencing joy and satisfaction in their current position. As an entrepreneur and the leader of the company, you can be of service to the employee.

I know of entrepreneurs who call other companies themselves to try to relocate certain employees. They look closely at the personality of the employee and the circumstances in which this employee can flourish and grow. They are looking for a company that fits well with that. Often, the employee prefers to look for another company himself but appreciates the offer.

In practice, communication turns out to be very important for a good relationship between employee and manager. Managing expectations is crucial. Consider personal development plans, reviews, and 360-degree feedback, performance, and assessment interviews.

When discussion and communication are no longer possible, in the best interests of the business and the other employees, the manager needs to choose dismissal. Dissatisfied employees are unhappy, often become troublemakers, and have a high level of absenteeism. Companies face a decline in quality and efficiency. Maintaining people in their position who are not functioning well can also become an excuse for others to do the same.

Love in business can sometimes be experienced or interpreted as a weakness. As a result, employees may think they can get away with quite a bit. The important thing is to realize that true love can also be expressed by firmness and setting boundaries. Love wants the other to grow, and when the other is taking advantage of what seems like a weakness, his character and development do not have the opportunity for growth.

It is comparable to raising children. You don't give them everything they want, but you help them grow up. This requires an upbringing in which a child learns to cope with boundaries and suffers consequences and setbacks. It is in a person's best interest to experience the consequences of his actions; this makes him mature and responsible. Sometimes a dismissal is the start of a healing process that begins with self-reflection about one's own successes or failures and, in this way, contributes to personal growth and development. When done this way, even a dismissal can be done in love—kind and compassionate, but with firm boundaries.

Painful Processes

It can be that we are forced to close down companies or business departments. How do we do justice to the different interests involved, and how can love work within these interests?

Let me tell you the story of the Jansen family business, which had to deal with an unprofitable department. This very department had once been the start of the business but had now become superfluous due to time and changes. Loyal employees who started alongside the founder of the business had been working in this department for 30–40 years. In the meantime, the founder's son, Tony, had taken over the business and worked with many of these people in his early years. How does one go about closing a department full of loyal employees who have taught you the trade? External advisors said *just close it*. It's an unavoidable part of the necessary process to get business going again.

Tony found this very difficult. He tried to start the process, attempting to keep his own emotions out of the decision. He no longer visited the department, he no longer wanted to talk to those employees, even sending his assistant if something had to be communicated. He hoped that in time, this would help make his decision easier, but the situation continued to be miserable. At one point, he concluded that his method wasn't working.

Tony was looking for a different way to let them go. He decided that closing himself off to emotions and human contact was the worst thing he could do. Tony realized that if he wanted to remain human, he could not deny love. This process hurt and was supposed to hurt. He came to the conviction that if he had to make this decision, he should be able to explain it not only to his employees but also must be able to share his reasoning with his employees' partners and families at their homes. That was the start of a process in which Tony sat his employees down one by one at the table, asking about all of their personal circumstances, options, and future possibilities. When it came to letting them go, maximum justice was done to the individual. Some were angry, some indignant, others happy. At that time, a lot of slander was spread about Tony. Now, years after the closure, Tony can still look everyone in the eye and he's slowly regained respect and appreciation, even from the people who were angry at the time.

A situation like this can also go in a very different direction, where the love and genuine care of the owner are not appreciated. I know of a similar situation. A department of a family business closed, the same department in which the business had started. The story is more or less the same, only at the moment when the personal conversations started, it began to go amiss. The employees, who remained angry despite the proposed arrangement, went to the trade union. The union resisted the arrangements made, insisting that everyone should be treated equally. Trade union leaders managed to get their hands on the employees, escalating the conflict within the company.

The newspapers got wind of it, and the case was picked up by the media. The owner of the business received negative publicity and was misrepresented. A general dismissal with severance pay took place. After that, everyone had to take care of his own, without help in shaping a new future. Relationships were disturbed, love was gone, and everyone involved had a bitter aftertaste. There was no better arrangement, no one felt understood, and there were no winners.

Acting out of love will not always result in smoother transitions. People of love don't love for the better results but for the sake of love itself. They do it because they desire to be a person of love. In this last situation, love made the entrepreneur cry. There were no winners in the end, but the ending didn't change his love or business behavior.

Sometimes the pain is inevitable. We as leaders must be willing to suffer for what is right. We know that in difficult situations, decisions are usually not understood and appreciated in the moment. But the worst thing that can happen in circumstances like forced layoffs and department closures is that you shut yourself off from the pain and emotions of the people around you, as well as your own. You need to endure this pain that comes as a side-effect of loving people if you want to dismiss people in a just and human way. Of course, you need advisors to make sure that it is done well and professionally, but the goal must be that all parties are done justice.

Love in Customer Relations

Obviously, there are two reasons to focus on satisfied and returning customers. We do this because we are intrinsically driven by *philia* love for the customer as a human being. This also means it's sincere and, therefore, good business. Philia love can mean that a successful sale is a result and a consequence of a sincere customer relationship.

With my background in selling high-end cars, I know the power of authentic and sincere customer relations. Whereas at the beginning of my career the focus was on pushing sales numbers, smart sales tricks, and the right closing techniques, this changed over the years to building and maintaining honest and authentic relationships. The result was that at a minimum, we sold the same numbers, but with higher profit margins and more fun.

Good car salespeople sell a car as a by-product of their personality. They may hear the customer upon leaving say, "Oh yes, go ahead and do the blue one." And so another car of more than €100,000 has been sold. I know salespeople for whom customers queue up on Saturdays to be helped by—not because they give better prices or deals to customers but because of the relationship. The other sellers, who were jealous and had less to do, asked these customers if they could help because they were available. The answer was invariably no. The relationship was decisive.

A study published in *The Harvard Business Review* shows that loyal and returning customers ensure higher profit margins and lower costs.[4] An increase of 5% in customer loyalty increases profits by 25%. Other figures from my past experience include the following: Attracting new customers costs about five times as much as retaining existing customers. Loyal customers, on average, are worth 33% more than other customers. They are also willing to pay more for services and are less price conscious. In addition, the chance that they buy new and follow-up products from you is 50% higher than other customers.

Another important effect is that loyal customers become ambassadors of your company. This is because almost half of American consumers say that the experiences of friends and acquaintances are the reason they choose a shop or a product.[5] The chance that these people actually make a purchase at the store in question is four times higher than at any other store, and the impact of a recommendation by friends is five times greater than any other advertisement or paid promo. This is a more-than-sufficient reason to work on customer satisfaction and retaining customers, I would say.

Relationships in the Times of Spreadsheets

Real business relationships remain important, even when spreadsheets and digitization increasingly decide control of the purchasing process.

Suppose you are a supplier to a large company and the purchasing process shifts from personal relationships to price and quality standards in spreadsheets. The buyers are changed every three years to prevent relationships from forming. The purchasing processes are determined by formal bids. Is it still possible that, even here, love and personal relationships matter?

It is certain that even in these markets, good relationships make all the difference. The trick is to be distinctive in the service provided based on a genuine interest in the customer and his needs. The challenge is to build the relationships that are needed repeatedly. These are needed to be able to make improvements and add visible value to the product and process before the policymakers send out a tender with the quotation criteria. Always think from the perspective of your customer and ask yourself how you can improve his profit or value proposition. The art of doing business is to connect your products or services with the interests of the customer in an economically profitable way for both. This requires an individual approach and knowing your customer and his needs.

The shared long-term interest is the starting point of the relationship. Innovation, cooperation, and modernization always develop through people and trustworthy relationships. Trust is the currency. Trust is proven by dedication and consistent behavior. Love can have a positive effect in this respect, and despite disappointments, it is important to keep love as the driver of your behavior to ensure that you continue to persevere and invest in the customer.

Take, for example, a large retailer, who wants to increase his profit margin by putting pressure on his suppliers. He sends a letter to all his suppliers to lower the price by 2%; otherwise, they would lose the contract and access to the retailer's shops. The ones who established a good relationship were able to discuss alternative products and concepts with this retailer. By offering new products and concepts, they were able to change the current sales mix in favor of these innovations and raise the turnover and margin of both the supplier and the retailer.

This was only possible because of the relationship. The others without a good relationship could only follow the new guideline set and lower their price by 2%. Sincere and long-term reliable relationships always pay off, even in a transparent market of Excel sheets and public tenders. Throughout these relationships, you can make a difference.

Another example that shows the usefulness of good relationships was a major producer who wanted to close his factory in a certain country and move it to a low-wage-earning country. A supplier who had maintained a good relationship with the director heard about this. The manufacturer still had all kinds of contracts running with various suppliers. He was afraid of lawsuits and problems arising, but the cost advantage of the new location made these temporary inconveniences affordable, according to him.

Of course, loving relationships require commitment from both parties. That is why it was important to make the benefits clear for both parties and to understand each other's win in this cooperation. Without a relationship, the supplier hoped for the highest possible compensation for breach of contract. With a good relationship, he worked on setting up a production unit as a supplier in that low-wage country as well, thereby increasing the profitability of both parties.

After a few meetings with this producer, it became clear that this was possible. The reliability of this supplier, his trustworthiness, and his performance was the basis of this new business relationship. But without this former relationship, he would not have been able to meet the owner and would never have heard of his plans of moving before it had happened.

These two characteristics, the trustworthy and reliable personal relationship and his outstanding performance in the past, created the confidence that allowed both to invest together in a new future. A relationship that was driven by love and based on performance and reliability was able to help secure the future of this specific supplier.

Love is also committed to excellent service and performance because love wants to give its best to the other.

Love in Difficult Situations

How do we love in a business relationship that is less than smooth? Do our principles still stand? Suppose you have a supplier who doesn't deliver on time or regularly delivers inferior quality. How do you deal with this from a loving point of view?

Love always first looks to the interests of the other without losing sight of his own interests. Love has to do with both interests and a healthy balance of giving and receiving. In a business relationship, the other is the client, the employee, and/or the supplier. When you love yourself in a healthy way, you can't accept when the other is not weighing your interests. This healthy love of self rejects abuse, poor service, and being provided with inferior quality products.

Some businesses increase their own profits through claims and lawsuits when there is a problem with a supplier. This is an example of only looking out for oneself. On the other hand, there are also businesses that, in the event of problems with the supplier, see opportunities to grow together. They engage in dialogue with the supplier, investigating together why things went wrong and trying to improve.

Some businesses advise their suppliers, working together on process improvement so that the desired quality and deadlines are met. Love works toward the growth and prosperity of everyone, including a failing supplier. Helping benefits all parties. The achieved improvements translate into better coordination, better integration of processes, more efficient work, and a better price.

Love may also mean saying goodbye to a supplier. With this finality, he is confronted with his own actions and manner of working. If people can discover their own strengths and weaknesses through your dealings with them and can learn and grow, then even this becomes an act of love. Of course, saying goodbye to suppliers only takes place after a process of discussions, negotiations, and written warnings so the supplier knows and understands why the working relationship is terminated.

Not only do clarity and communication often prevent misplaced claims and negative feelings, but they give insight into where the supplier could improve in the future. We must feel that we have done everything that could reasonably be expected of us to enable a supplier to adapt to new market conditions or higher quality requirements.

Love in Business

Entrepreneurship done in love flavors life and gives it meaning. For me, God is the ultimate source and reason for love. If you have come to know the *agape* love of God, it becomes a well within you that wants to flow toward others and serves them for their own well-being. This kind of love is possibly not understood by others. Love is tender and can cause you pain when you are being misunderstood or mistreated. Masculine love can be tough, too, but when balanced with empathy and a sincere interest in the well-being of others, it is the best instrument to help others grow and become resilient.

The Christian Jerusalem entrepreneur loves for the sake of love. Since love is a well from within, it is powerful and can endure anything. This love is persistent and gives hope and faith. This kind of love has given me life and meaning and flavors my life richly as an entrepreneur. It makes me want to serve my fellow man and has become the basis of my business mission. I have discovered that there are two important prerequisites for expressing love well: being in connection and understanding who the other is.

14

Connection Within Business

Connected living is one of the characteristics of the Jerusalem entrepreneur. We don't live for ourselves; we are part of something bigger. We can have various forms of connection; for example, we live in connection with our inner being, our values, our emotions, with God, with creation, with society, and with other human beings. We are relational beings.

Resilience and Rootedness

Most people and entrepreneurs try to influence and control circumstances and their relationships for their own benefit and well-being. Therefore, they focus on their relationship to circumstances and others, first. But why is being connected to yourself important? How will this help in our quest for well-being and what will this look like at a company level?

The coronavirus crisis taught many entrepreneurs the importance of being resilient. Resilience means having the ability to deal with surprises, changes, and unexpected setbacks in a healthy manner.[1] In the future, it will be even more important because this crisis will not be the last one. We have faced many in the past, such as the financial crisis in 2008, and we will face more crises and turmoil over time sparked by a variety of factors, such as new innovations, disruptive technologies, war, or other catastrophes. We need to be prepared. Therefore, many companies will shift their focus from efficiency to resilience.

Excellence and efficiency are the basics for staying in the game, but they are presupposed by our clients. Delivery on-demand, without mistakes and in time, is and will be the new excellence in serving our clients. The client is expecting us to deliver everything at his doorstep without mistakes and at the lowest price. The lowest price will be determined by the efficiency and excellence we can develop and not by a lower quality. How does resilience play into this?

Resilient people and companies operate from what is within. They can overcome changing external influences by their inner strength and not by controlling the external circumstances. They can view circumstances differently because they know who they are and why they exist. The Christian Jerusalem entrepreneur has even external powers and sources available, such as God's presence, promises, peace, and a secure future. This enables him to move in the changed circumstances and become a power for good because he doesn't live for himself.

VUCA Society

Our environment is rapidly evolving. As leaders in such a dynamic society, we can no longer control everything. So, how to be an entrepreneur and a leader in today's world?

Our world today is sometimes referred to as VUCA, as in VUCA-society or -world.[2] The acronym VUCA stands for the chaotic, fast-paced times in which we live. The individual letters stand for:

- *V = Volatility:* The unpredictability and rapidity of change. Technology and social media are transforming the world and our behavioral patterns, as can a pandemic, war, or a political statement.
- *U = Uncertainty:* The uncertainty about what is about to happen. The speed of the increase in knowledge is tremendous. Our total knowledge doubles approximately 12 months. In the medical field, it is expected that knowledge will double every 73 days before 2021.[3] What is true today and what is considered the right treatment may be outdated tomorrow and better diagnosed with new techniques. An example of this is the use of Watson, an IBM supercomputer.[4] A doctor bases his choices on previous findings and experiences. Within milliseconds, Watson looks at millions of articles and perceptions of the subject—more than anything a person could ever remember. Watson interprets the data entered and uses it to provide an overview of the expected diagnosis and treatment with the best results.

  In the business world, *disruptive* is the buzzword for the search for new innovations in the earning models of businesses. New earning models are making others redundant.

  Uncertainty is the thing that entrepreneurs fear the most. We are used to moving and being active, but if we don't know in which direction the world is moving, it is hard to make decisions. A survey[5] in April 2020 amid the coronavirus crisis showed that the greatest challenge CEOs are facing is *uncertainty* (37%), next to cash flow (25%), profitable revenue growth (16%), employee care (14%), and peer interaction (8%). We can only overcome uncertainty with vision. A vision that is rooted in our identity helps us navigate in times of uncertainty.

- *C = Complexity:* The multitude of forces, chaos, and confusion around us. We are so connected to each other and the world that a small event somewhere far away can have a huge impact on our existence here. A small economic decision in China can have far-reaching consequences for our economy. War in the Middle East can raise oil prices and disrupt the global economy. A drought in Africa can raise food prices and lead to uprisings in all kinds of countries, which, in turn, affects our economy and political stability.
- *A = Ambiguity:* The cause and effect are unclear and difficult to explain. There is a lot of fake news and misinformation. The result is that people become cynical and indifferent. People withdraw into their own world of perception and truth.

Navigating in uncertain times

To overcome the threat of volatility, we need to understand our calling and identity. These can direct us in volatile times.

To overcome uncertainty, we need to have a clear purpose and vision that can guide us in these times of uncertainty. Next to our values and principles as being a part of our purpose.

To overcome complexity, we need to learn to act out of love. Love is the guiding principle in times of uncertainty.

To overcome ambiguity and to help us to understand we need the questions 'who' and 'why'. Who is telling us what and why?

To make quick and decisive choices in such a VUCA society, your company needs a strong foundation and agility. This foundation should consist of two building blocks:

1. Your identity and calling as an entrepreneur and the purpose, vision, and values of the company.
2. The resilience of your business and its organization

Agile
Your ability to adapt and evolve in a changing market is determined by the following building blocks below:

Identity and Values as Foundation Block 1	**Resilience as Foundation Block 2**
• Why does your company exist? • Who do you want to be, and which values determine your business philosophy and actions? • Is this fully integrated into your business culture and does everyone experience it?	• How much cash and financial reserve is available? • What quality of people do you have? • What is your innovation capacity and abilities? • Is your organization prepared to make decisions on various levels?

A healthy company in a VUCA society can quickly adapt to changing circumstances.

Purpose, Vision, Identity and Values

To be agile, it is very important to know where you are going; otherwise, you will just run around. Therefore, it is important to have a clear vision and know who you are as a company. A company must develop a purpose and vision that is bigger than the business itself.

The purpose and vision should inspire and guide everything that the business does. We know that when employees feel connected to business objectives, they experience more meaning and perform better. Staying true to this vision is important.

As a leader, staying true to your objectives is one of the most important pillars of the human capital of business. A study by Bruno Roche from the company Mars shows that the connection the manager has with the values and objectives of business is one of the most important components for the well-being of the staff. It's determined by the ability of the manager to "walk the talk" regarding values.[6]

Other important elements for the growth of the human capital are the following: the level of trust, social cohesion, and the possibility of cooperation with the manager. The relationship with the line manager is very decisive in employee self-confidence, productivity, quality level, and involvement.

These ways of connecting management and employees appear to be crucial for the well-being of the staff, lead to positive consequences for profitability, and set the climate within the business. Good relationships contribute to a business's financial, human, social, and spiritual capital.

Your identity is formed by being known and loved, and living based on clear values and guiding principles, which, regardless of the circumstances, give life direction. It is important to know who you are—as an individual as well as a company—and what you stand for.

The company's identity is formed by its mission and vision, which reflects the reason the company exists. This shapes its purpose, goals, and culture. In a VUCA world, mission, vision, values, and culture are your foundation. They help you to navigate times of uncertainty because they give you stability and direction.[7]

If our company's identity and desired culture are rooted and all the people are connected to these two elements of the company, then we can evolve and change more easily, without losing ourselves and our goals. We can then stay the course, without being determined by the circumstances. What we do remains meaningful, despite the circumstances. Agility needs to be directed by a vision, full of purpose and meaning, and carried by a culture based on the clear identity and values of the company.

Connected to the Objectives

Why do we do the things we do? There's a well-known expression that says, *"Making money is killing your business."*[8] The focus on money causes us to break away from our roots and from our company's original goal of serving the customer. We are then no longer building business by focusing on excellence and quality service. Business as an instrument of blessing disappears from sight.

In this focus on money only, it is also possible that an entrepreneur regularly changes course because he believes he can earn more money in other markets. I knew of such an entrepreneur. Due to the rapid turnarounds and loss of focus, a sustainable company was not built. The customers became estranged from the business because they no longer knew what it stood for, while employees became disenchanted from the business because they no longer knew what the purpose of the business was.

Middle management could no longer give direction or was hesitant to do so. Customers and employees could no longer connect with the business's vision because they no longer knew what it stood for. Such a thing can really happen to a beautiful and well-running company. This company, once able to buy other businesses, was now bought out by another company. Profits had tanked and shareholders, customers, and staff had lost confidence in the business.

We should be careful of the temptation of making money the purpose of the company because it is a strong power and will influence our thinking and behavior. Too much and too often we fall for this power. What can help you stay free of this love for money is a daily devotional time, a time of the day you dedicate to God, reflecting on your actions, as well as a good board of directors or an accountability group.

Money is an important means to an end but making money can never become the purpose of the company.

A Resilient Company

To become agile as a company, we need to have resilient resources as well. This means that our resources help us cope with surprises, changes, and unexpected setbacks. I distinguish four types of resources within a company that are important for becoming agile and resilient: finances, the eco-system, people, and the organization.

Finances. We as a company must have an adequate cash flow, free equity, and low and manageable debt. We know the phrases, 'cash is king' and 'turn-over is vanity, profit is sanity, cash is reality'.

Ecosystem. Ecosystems are communities and relationships where we can work together with each other as specialists in our own field of expertise. In this way we can do both with more speed: generating innovative solutions and successfully executing them. We cannot limit ourselves by our own expertise. For our company to be resilient, it is important to have access to good resources, such as knowledge, networks of companies, and knowledge centers that share technology, information, and good employees.

People. Good employees are people who have the potential to develop themselves. We as entrepreneurs must empower our employees so they can make the right decisions at the right time. For this reason, employees must be connected to the identity and values of a business so they can make the right decisions.

Organization. A good organization should be able to stimulate and lead to employee development. All of this means that businesses can hold their own in a changing market.

A Teal Organization

A special type of organization that fits well with this is what Frederic Laloux calls a "teal organization."[9] What kind of organization is this?

First, there is self-direction and self-organization. There are no managers, and the staff decides together, in teams, how to flesh out the work. They are motivated by the values and objectives of business.

In my opinion, three things are very important in this model of self-management:

1. That the positive and negative consequences of the decisions are carried by the individual or the team and not by something or someone else.
2. That there are strong guiding frameworks that are anchored in processes (ICT).
3. That we have mature and qualified employees who believe in and personify the values and purpose of the business.

Second, there is talk of *wholeness*. This means that the whole person is involved in the work. Next to the use of his mind and logic, his emotional, spiritual, male, or female side play a part in the execution of the job as well. In this concept, everyone can contribute in his own way and be himself. Interconnected and aligned people make everything more beautiful and complete.

Third, at the moment of important decisions, all parties concerned are consulted. This gives a wider perspective than just the personal interest of the department.

"In the new organizations, management becomes a way to really bring out the best in people, where trust is given and where work is done based on a common human interest. This creates working environments that are inspiring, goal-oriented, and productive," says Laloux in the business magazine *Management Team*.[10]

A "teal organization" is focused on connection at every level. In this type of organization, employees and people are connected with themselves and their team, to the purpose and goals of the business, and with all the stakeholders. Decision-making occurs when all decisions in the organization are made by those involved. The interests of all stakeholders are weighed by those who have to make the decision, therefore involving all in the decision without leading to bureaucracy. A good example of a "teal organization" in the Netherlands is the Buurtzorg company,[11] as Laloux describes in his book.[12]

Being Connected: A Key to Success

Focusing on the connections inside the company helps it to survive, to become stronger, to be agile, and to be resilient. But this can never be a goal in itself. A company derives its raison d'être from solving the problems and needs of clients and fulfilling the wishes of people. Companies consist of people. Clients are human beings. Through my encounter with the other, my world becomes bigger than my own thoughts and perceptions. The art of entrepreneurship is to be connected in such a way with others that I know how I can bless all parties.

As long as I, as the entrepreneur, still have an abstract idea of business, I will continue to think in numbers and objectives and lose the connection with real life, while missing the opportunity of being a source of well-being. Next to that, I also lose the perspective of being a person after the image and likeness of Christ. Numbers and goals are not the reason for business; they are only a tool to help businesses flourish and serve people to the best of my abilities.

15

Earning Models

Babylon's earning model focuses on destruction. Nimrod expands by killing and eliminating the competition. Optimization is done by force. Value is found in self-interest and consumption.

The earning model put into the creation and that works with the values of the New Jerusalem is different. In this model, expansion takes place by taking care of the means of living and business and adding value to the product/service to increase profit and value for the customer. This model adds value to the common good and community.

Multiplication is sharing.

The great principle of multiplication is sharing. We can apply this to our current business operations. This is at odds with our calculation methods and way of thinking, but it is an old law. It is a principle that says that ten minus five is not equal to five but is a multiple of ten, maybe even a hundred or more. This is God's principle, one which is closely connected with his order of creation and his Kingdom.

The idea is simple: if we want something to grow, we give it away or share it. In other words, we invest. The investment is optimized through care and attention. Here are a few examples.

A Grain of Corn

If we want a kernel to bear fruit, we plant it in the ground. The automatic multiplying principle is the germinating power that God has placed into this grain and into the properties of the earth. The seed bears fruit—10, 20, 30 times or more—and offers an unstoppable yield. If we care for the soil by plowing and fertilizing, we increase the yield. Work, care, and attention is our contribution to the potential that God has placed in creation, down to a grain.

Intangible Values

Intangible values also grow by being given away. Take love, for example. If we don't share love, it dies. When we share love, it multiplies for the one who shares as well as for the one who receives. The person receiving love wants to share it with others. That is the automatism principle that God has put into the immaterial values. Of course, this multiplication principle also applies to destructive values, such as hatred. It's important then to pay attention to what we are multiplying. Optimization happens when we invest good values in capable people who, in turn, share these values.[1]

Skills and Talents

The multiplication principle for growth through sharing also applies to our talents and skills. If we want to multiply them and let them bear fruit, then we must train and practice them. Take a carpenter, for example. The more he practices his craft, the more skilled he becomes. He grows in his profession by practicing his profession. Research shows that if you want to grow from an apprentice to a professional, it takes about 5,000 hours of practical practice and work.[2] That's about three to four years of dedicated work. Then the same time is asked again to grow into being a master of your profession, someone who can teach others. After that, you might be able to develop into an artist in your field. As an artist, you can challenge and change the existing conventions in your specific field of study due to your professionalism and expertise.

All this requires love, time, care, and attention for your profession. Exercising and making your talent available to the client enables you to develop and grow. In this way, the customer and society benefit from your growth process. This is a double profit. As an expert, you may be able to help an entire industry with new innovations and production methods that were previously unthinkable. However, if you don't do anything with your talent and don't share anything, nobody will benefit. And neither will you. Optimization takes place through dedication and practice.

Knowledge

Sharing knowledge and experiences causes multiplication. If we share knowledge, others can build on our shared knowledge and experiences. Then you, as the originator, will be able to build on the new input of others. In this way, we grow and accumulate knowledge. If we share this knowledge worldwide, we can make knowledge grow and mutually benefit from the help of others worldwide. The consequences are new innovations and new technologies, including those who are the first to make the knowledge available. Everyone benefits. Prosperity and well-being grow as a result of this increase in knowledge.

By sharing information and knowledge, this hypothetical sector has become a world leader in its field. Think also of the new university campuses; not only students are trained there, but businesses are also setting up innovation, research, and development centers. Companies share their information with students, and students, in turn, with businesses. In addition to these centers, there are also rooms and buildings where startups on the brink of new developments can establish themselves and try to convert their knowledge into business and earning models. These combinations of knowledge, science, business, and creativity help a country grow economically.

Finances

Financially, the growth principle remains intact—when we invest our money in good people and businesses, everyone benefits. If we distribute money by investing in businesses and new developments, the money can grow and pay off. Investing money carefully and remaining attentive to the people related to our investments is crucial for healthy growth. On the other side, we know that the accumulation of money in only a few hands hampers economic growth and leads to stagnation and scarcity. Sharing money throughout investments in real businesses helps the common good flourish because it provides jobs and wealth.

Even sharing risks throughout cooperation and shared projects pay. The law of large numbers allows us to better handle risk. By sharing risks in new investments, we become bolder and dare to take up an advance on the expected and coming benefits and profit of projects. This helps to realize dreams, big projects, and developments. We can do more together than alone.

Investing Your Money Well

If we want to multiply our money by investing in businesses, it requires commitment, care, and attention for the people in whom we want to invest money. This may seem logical, but it is often not put into practice.

Banks, based on their professional obligation, are less likely to invest in risky businesses, start-ups, or certain entrepreneurial adventurous opportunities. This creates opportunities for private and involved investors who are willing to take risks by investing in businesses and entrepreneurial people with talent. An important question for the private investor is, "Can I as an investor make a meaningful contribution to this project?" Here, several arguments can play a role. Perhaps it's important to us as investors to give a young entrepreneur the opportunity to start his adventure. Maybe we want to support important social developments, or maybe we see the investment as aiding development.

It's only when the investor can answer this question positively that he begins to add value to the business with his abilities, talents, and knowledge. A committed investor is good for business if he has long-term business interests in mind and shares the values of the business or the owner.

Healthy private investors, driven by a vision and with long-term interests, are a blessing for the economy and for businesses. They work on the basis of added value and reciprocity. They are not interested in power but want to contribute to the jointly formulated interests of business and society. These are a Jerusalem investor's qualities; he is considerately involved in the investment not only for his own share but because of his belief in the cause and the people behind it.

A Babylon investor, by contrast, thinks first and foremost about the return of the investment, the part that matters most to him. He puts the business's management under pressure, making his own interests as an investor the center of the business operations. Such an investor can, for example, order costs to be reduced, insisting that R&D (research and development) closes, that charitable projects must stop, that new technologies must not be developed, or that the business must be divided and sold.

From the perspective of the entrepreneur looking for foreign capital who wants to raise extra capital by allowing additional shareholders or investors to take part in his company, it is incredibly important that he only works with parties that share the same values and the same long-term vision for the business. Paul speaks about this when he warns of being unequally yoked.[3] In my application, Paul is warning against partners working and thinking from two different sets of values. In my experience, this goes wrong in many collaborations. For a Christian Jerusalem entrepreneur who has given God the ownership of the business, collaboration with a non-Christian at this level is impossible; how can he listen to the voice of God if his partner does not agree? We cannot serve two masters, nor can we live in separate worlds.

An IPO?

Sharing the same values is essential for a healthy long-term relationship. For example, you may ask yourself whether it is wise for a Christian entrepreneur to have his company listed on the stock exchange, where all shares or a majority of the shares are offered. Of course, an IPO (a company's Initial Public Offering) provides the owner with cash and extra business capital. But if you offer a majority of the shares or do not build in anti-takeover constructions, you no longer have control over your company.

Some Babylonian investors have only one interest, and that is profit maximization and shareholder value. In an IPO where a Christian owner loses his ownership, questions must be asked. As a Christian, you sell the soul of your company to mammon if you lose ownership through an IPO. It is better to have slow and sustainable growth on your own or with committed private investors than to have quick capital from the stock market with an investor who is driven by different interests and values than your own.

Working Together and Cooperation

Old wisdom is "many hands, make light work." Working together pays in better and more growth than working alone. For example, if we use each other's expertise, we can do more. If we start to specialize in one particular field, our knowledge will grow deeper. So if we can cooperate and work together with many specialists, we have more profound knowledge available. The more we differ from each other, the more potential there is for growth, innovation, and new developments. So differences need to be valued. Cooperation enables us to use our differences to strengthen each other, to specialize, and to grow. If we work together, our profit is no longer the loss of someone else, but we mutually benefit. In this way, economy is no longer a science of scarcity but of abundance.

To practice this, we need a change of attitude, to get away from the fear of losing power, and to get away from the thinking of scarcity and move into the thinking of abundance and trust. In the latter thinking, we are no longer each other's competitors, but partners.

Requirements for growth throughout cooperation are:

- The individual is willing to take the whole picture into account. He is focused on the greater good and keeps in mind all costs, all benefits, and all the stakeholders.
- All the profits and benefits are shared with all stakeholders. Everyone gets compensated for his contribution to the whole.
- The awareness that everything of value is fragile and vulnerable, and that even the weakest has inherent worth. Everyone needs to be included and honored.
- Mutuality is a basic principle of growth through cooperation. There must be a win-win.
- The most important and non-negotiable aspect of cooperation and working together is to live the principle of trust to the ultimate end, even when it harms you, because trust is the currency of

trading, business, and wealth. In low-trust companies and societies, people are imprisoned in fear and scarcity and will not deliver themselves to the greater good. They will focus only on their own interests by keeping control and enlarging influence by power and submitting others.

- To foster and maintain cooperation for growth, we need leadership in the company that rules with justice and righteousness, even protecting the weak. With the absence of strong and just leadership, a corporation or company can easily change into a robber-gang where everyone lives and works for himself alone, sparking the collapse of the corporation or company itself.

Adding Value

As an entrepreneur, we can add value on various levels. We can add value to a product, to existing services, and to the customer as one of the stakeholders of the company.
The concept of adding value to a product is that a company does something to increase the value of a certain product to contribute to the needs of the customer. The profit of the company comes from the difference between the price of the finished product/service and the cost of the inputs involved in making it.

We can add value to a product in various ways. This can be done by building a brand, delivering excellent service, product features and benefits, offering convenience, etc. If we can translate the customer's needs into our talents and possibilities, then we have a business concept.

The Christian Jerusalem entrepreneur doesn't want to add value for profit alone but because he wants to contribute to the well-being of the customer. He doesn't only try to add value to his product for better sales and profit but also to add value to the life of the customer for his or her well-being. We can do this in various ways. We can do it through our products being useable and needed. We can do it through our services, making life more comfortable, sustainable, or healthy. We can do it through the way we make the products, by a sustainable circular production method, or by technological innovation.

We can do it through the taxes we pay, which are contributing to the greater good and society and, therefore, to the well-being of the individual. We can do it by being generous, by supporting social projects, and by contributing to charity. We can do it through the jobs we create for people, giving them an income. Adding value in all its facets optimizes the multiplication model of "sharing." We share our talents, skills, resources, and company with society to contribute to well-being and the greater good in an economical way.

Our right to exist as a company is determined by the value we add to products, services, and customers. Opposite to this model of adding value is the model of harvesting. Instead of investing, we are only taking, just as Nimrod did. Harvesting is about creating monopolies to raise prices, fooling the customer, selling insurances he doesn't need, speculating on the stock exchange and with financial papers, and avoiding paying legal taxes.

These ways of making money don't contribute to the value of the product, the service, or the customers' well-being. The model of adding value, seen by Melchizedek, is much more productive than the model of harvesting, as we saw with Nimrod. If we only harvest the soil repeatedly, the soil will become poor, but if we plow, sow, and fertilize, we create wealth and a sustainable future. Adding value is the model for a healthy future.

16

Becoming a Christian Jerusalem Entrepreneur

We have made quite the journey in this book. We discussed what forms your identity as an entrepreneur and learned about two opposing spiritual powers and ways of doing business. We have discovered that the Jerusalem entrepreneur is someone who feels called to co-create with God in the world of business for the greater good and to the glory of God, while the Babylonian entrepreneur's model is based on ego with the goal of eliminating competition and building a personal utopia.

The Christian Jerusalem entrepreneur is not driven by profit maximization but by his contribution to the well-being of those involved in his company. Secular businessmen can run their businesses with the same values as a Jerusalem entrepreneur, while Christian entrepreneurs can get caught up in a Babylonian mentality of doing business. The point is that God wants to be present and rule in us with the power of the Holy Spirit as we do business in this world. Out of this connection with God, God Himself will transform us to become more like him. He will establish this (New) Jerusalem, despite our efforts.

Why become a Christian Jerusalem entrepreneur?

If God will build the New Jerusalem himself, why become a Christian Jerusalem entrepreneur? Because we are called. Our love for God and humanity drives us to see good come to fruition, although we know that this path will also be difficult.

A good friend once asked a group of Christian entrepreneurs why they were investing in a remote, impoverished area of Europe. After all, their group alone couldn't change this poor nation with their limited investment. These Christian businesspeople answered, "Our approach may be limited in its effectiveness to change the nation but is very effective for the few we reach by our limited efforts. Ask about the impact of our work on those who are changed by it. We are not trying to save the world; that's God's task. We are doing this for them." It was and is the love of Christ that compels them. We are not Christian Jerusalem entrepreneurs because it makes us success stories but because we cannot do otherwise. Becoming a Christian Jerusalem entrepreneur is being gripped by something much larger than yourself: Jesus' love for humanity.

When we start to understand and practice this, people will discover the power in our lives, which is beyond human understanding. Next to the immediate effect of doing good, we hope sincerely that our way of acting will intrigue the spectators. That they will start to ask questions we can answer at the right time and at the right moment, as we are always willing to give an account of our faith.

A good friend of mine in a Muslim nation in these COVID-19 months was running out of cash and was praying to God for new streams of cash to keep his company and witness going. He denied himself a personal income, although his family was suffering because he was trying to be a reliable partner and trustworthy business owner as a Christian in a Muslim society. Every month, a miracle took place to bridge the expenses to the next month. Unexpected governmental subsidies were coming in, new clients paid in advance, and some allowed temporary payment delays because they were impressed by the behavior of this entrepreneur.

People saw his faith put into practice, which sparked many conversations because he was open about his faith. I don't know the end of his story, but I am impressed by my friend's dedication and the way he witnesses in these times of crisis. For me, he is a great example of being a Christian Jerusalem entrepreneur. He works toward his society's well-being, he gives God the glory, and everyone who recognizes his actions responds. It is amazing what God can do.

You will have your own story as you put your faith into action and its principles into your business. Welcome to the adventurous life of being a Christian Jerusalem entrepreneur working in partnership with God and co-creating in the world of business for the greater good and God's glory.

Afterword

In this book, I have tried to explain how and why the Jerusalem entrepreneur is far more preferable than the Babylon entrepreneur. Maybe as a reader, you didn't agree with everything I argued or some ideas were far from your own worldview. I do hope, however, that you have become inspired to discover the New Jerusalem.

My desire is that you can experience God's tangible nearness and presence. He is the God who continues to make all things new. He is the God who wants to draw close to humanity. Therefore, we can live from grace, with open hands. It is through this God, the God of Israel; the God of Abraham, Isaac, and Jacob; and the God and Father of our Lord Jesus Christ, that we have hope and a future. It is in this God, the builder of the new earth and the New Jerusalem, that we are safe and secure. He alone deserves all the glory.

Thank you for reading, and may you experience a new richness in your entrepreneurship.

Endnotes

Introduction

[1] As opposed to egocentricity and narcissistic self-interest without taking the interest of others into account.

[2] https://europartners.org/

[3] As opposed to egocentricity and narcissistic self-interest without taking the interest of others into account.

Chapter 1: Two Cities: Babylon and Jerusalem

[1] Genesis 10: 8-12

[2] https://en.wikipedia.org/wiki/Babylon

[3] Genesis 14:18

[4] https://en.wikipedia.org/wiki/Jerusalem

[5] Revelation 17:4-5

[6] Revelation 18:7

[7] Genesis 1:26-29; Psalm 8

[8] Matthew 25:31-46

[9] Revelation 21

[10] 2 Chronicles 6:6; Psalm 48; 68:17; 78:68-69; 87; 132:13

[11] John 14: 15-20; 23

[12] Revelation 21:2, 9

[13] Compare 2 Corinthians 11:2 and Ephesians 5:21-32

[14] Revelation 21:2, 9

[15] Revelation 21:19. The stones and a foundation are under the ground. There is no point in covering them with gemstones. For me, we are talking about inner beauty.

[16] Galatians 5:22-24

[17] Revelation 19:8

[18] Revelation 21:3-4

[19] Isaiah 65:17; Revelation 21:4b

[20] Isaiah 60:18

[21] Isaiah 60:3; Revelation 21:24

[22] Isaiah 60:11; Revelation 21:25-26

[23] Revelation 21:2-4, 9

[24] John 3:16 and 1 John 4:8-10

[25] 1 Corinthians 13:4-7

[26] Introduction from C.S. Lewis, *The Four Loves*, Thomas Nelson Publishers, 2017, and a paper by van Bas van Os, "The things we do for love," April 2019 (in progress).

[27] Matthew 22:36-40

[28] Matthew 22:37-40

[29] Isaiah 54:14

[30] Romans 3:21-26

[31] Isaiah 61:1-3

[32] Luke 1:51-53

[33] Psalm 9 and 72; Luke 4:18-19

[34] Isaiah 11:3-4

[35] We see examples in Isaiah 11 and 65

[36] Genesis 10:8-12

[37] Genesis 10:8

[38] Dr. David Livingstone, a famous archaeologist (http://davelivingston.com/index.htm), compares Nimrod with Gilgamesh, who was incredibly cruel, arrogant, and a tyrant. He described him as a vile, filthy, perverted person, a rebel against God. http://davelivingston.com/nimrod.htm

[39] Flavius Josephus, in his work *The Antiquities of the Jews*, describes Nimrod as a tyrant (https://penelope.uchicago.edu/josephus/ant-1.html). "Now it was Nimrod who excited them to such an affront and contempt of God. He was the grandson of Ham, the son of Noah: a bold man, and of great strength of hand. He persuaded them not to ascribe it to God, as if it was through his means that they were happy; but to believe that it was their own courage that procured that happiness. He also gradually changed the government into a tyranny; seeing no other way of turning men from the fear of God, but to bring them into a constant dependence on his own power. He also said, "He would be revenged on God, if he should have a mind to drown the world again: for that he would build a Tower too high for the waters to be able to reach; and that he would avenge himself on God for destroying their fore-fathers." Book 1, Chapter 4, verse 2.

[40] See the time before the flood in Genesis 6:5.

[41] Genesis 10:8. Nimrod was the first ruler, mighty man, using power according to the Dutch translation of the Hebrew text. He builds the great cities of the east and a huge kingdom. The consequence of being the first is that it was not seen before. Hence, the conclusion that he was the first one using power and might to subjugate people and build kingdoms and civilizations in this way, with power and violence.

[42] Genesis 11:1-9

[43] Genesis 11:4

[44] Psalm 8: 6-7; Genesis 1:26-30

[45] Genesis 14:18-20

[46] Hebrews 5:2

[47] Genesis 14:19

[48] Genesis 13:2; 23:6

[49] Genesis 17:4; Romans 4:1

[50] 1 Peter 2:9

[51] 2 Corinthians 5:18 and 20

[52] 1 Peter 2:4-5, 9-10

[53] Genesis 11:9b

[54] Revelation 17: 6-15

[55] Revelation 17:15-17

[56] Revelation 18:8

[57] Revelation 18:10, 16-17, 19

[58] Revelation 17:18; 18:8-9, 21

[59] Isaiah 60: 3, 17b, Revelation 21:24-25

[60] Isaiah 65:17-18; Revelation 21:1-2

[61] 2 Corinthians 4:7

Chapter 2: Doing Business in a Babylonian Culture

[1] Daniel 1:1-2

[2] Daniel 1:3-4

[3] Daniel 2:48-49

[4] Deuteronomy 18:9-14

[5] Daniel 6:3

[6] Daniel 4:34

[7] Daniel 6:27-28

[8] Daniel 1:8

[9] Daniel 1

[10] Philippians 2:7-11

[11] Daniel 6

[12] Read the story in Daniel 6.

[13] A story from my friend Peter Briscoe, which was published in Europartners' young professional training.

[14] 1 Peter 2:12

[15] 1 Peter 2:19-20

[16] Jeremiah 29:4-7

[17] To Jeremiah 29:11-14

[18] Chapter 1, Melchizedek

[19] Jeremiah 29:7

[20] Matthew 5:16

[21] Matthew 25:14-30

[22] Matthew 25:31-46

[23] Chapter 1: Two Cities: Babylon and Jerusalem

[24] Matthew 5:14-16

Chapter 3: Who Are We?

[1] https://en.wikipedia.org/wiki/Henri_Nouwen

[2] https://www.youtube.com/watch?v=Uzna1FL8Syo

[3] For further reading: Arie de Rover, *Struck by Grace*, Buijten & Schipperheijn, 2014.

[4] Inspired by: Erik Borgman, *Leven van wat komt,* Meinema, 2017.

Chapter 4: One Who Is Called

[1] This is the first characteristic in the sequence of essential characteristics of a Christian Jerusalem entrepreneur.

[2] 2 Chronicles 1:7-10

[3] Viktor E. Frankl, *Man's Search for Meaning*, Donker, 1978.

[4] Viktor Frankl was a survivor of the Holocaust and is known as the founder of Logotherapy. His book, *Man's Search for Meaning,* illustrates his experiences as a prisoner in a concentration camp and describes his psychological method for finding the meaning of life in all life situations and, therefore, a reason to keep living.

[5] Genesis 1:26-28

[6] Genesis 2:15

[7] Matthew 7:12

[8] Matthew 22:37-40

[9] John 15; 1-7; John 17:20-23; 1 Corinthians 1:9

[10] John Piper, *Don't Waste Your Life*, Gideon, 2008.

[11] See Epilogue.

[12] Genesis 2:2 and 2:15

[13] Romans 8:29; 2 Corinthians 3:18b

[14] Galatians 5:22-23

[15] 2 Corinthians 5:20

[16] Exodus 3:14

[17] Hebrews 2:17-18, 4:14-16

[18] Matthew 24:45-51 and 25:14-46

[19] Luke 22:24-28; John 13:1-17

[20] Genesis 1:24

[21] Genesis 2:15

[22] Philippians 2:5-8

[23] Philippians 2:5-8

[24] Luke 22:25-26

[25] John 13

[26] Genesis 1:28

[27] Genesis 12:2; 15:5; 17:2-6

[28] John 8:39

[29] John 8:41-45

[30] Romans 4; Galatians 3 and 4

[31] Galatians 3:6-7

[32] 1 John 4:7

[33] Deuteronomy 6:7, 20-25

[34] Matthew 28:18-20; Mark 16:15-18; Luke 24:46-49 and John 20:20-23

[35] 2 Corinthians 3:2-3

[36] 2 Corinthians 5:20

[37] https://www.rlhymersjr.com/Articles/12-22-02Decendants.html

[38] 1 Corinthians 13:1-3

[39] Genesis 2:15-16

[40] See Prologue: Two cities: Babylon and Jerusalem under the paragraph "Loving Relationships: Connection and Service."

[41] Matthew 22:37-38. Also, see Mark 12:30; Luke 10:27

[42] 1 Corinthians 13:7

[43] 1 Corinthians 13:8; 1 John 4:16-17

[44] John 21:15-22

[45] Romans 12:3-9

[46] Europartners (https://europartners.org/) and Xpand (https://xpand.eu/) are offering several tools.

[47] John 15: 1-10

[48] John 15:8

[49] John 17:20-26; 1 Corinthians 1:9

Chapter 5: Living in Connection

[1] The Christian entrepreneur wants a connected life. He knows how to connect with God, his neighbor, himself, the world, and his ideals.

[2] Matthew 5:20-48

[3] Matthew 5:21-22

[4] Matthew 5:27-28

[5] Matthew 5:48

[6] Think, for example, of the general feeling of unease that emerging populist leaders have been successfully harvesting in recent years. (2017–2019).

[7] 1 John 4:18

Chapter 6: Love as the Foundation

[1] John 3:16

[2] John 4:14; 16; 19

[3] John 4:13-14; 7:38

[4] Matthew 22:36-38

[5] 1 John 4:17

Chapter 7: Performance Drive

[1] Europartners.org and CBMC are facilitating this in various nations.

Chapter 8: Entrepreneurial Qualities

[1] Stephen R. Covey, *The Seven Qualities of Effective Leaders*, Business Contact, 2010.

[2] Matthew 25:14-30; 1 Corinthians 3:9b-15

[3] 1 Samuel 13:14; Acts 13:22

[4] 1 Samuel 13; 15; 18:6-8

[5] Psalm 63:1-4

[6] Examples could be Psalm 27:4-5; 36:8-10; 42; 63

[7] John 4:23; John 15:4-7

[8] From John 15:4-17

[9] Psalm 23

[10] Psalm 18

[11] Psalm 90

[12] Psalm 91

[13] Psalm 121

[14] Psalm 139

[15] 1 Samuel 24, specifically verse 13

[16] 2 Samuel 11 and 12

[17] 2 Samuel 23:38

[18] 2 Samuel 11:14-17

[19] 1 Samuel 17:37; Psalm 18:30

[20] Psalm 51:12-13

[21] Matthew 10:16

[22] Proverbs 4:23

[23] https://tonyschocolonely.com/nl/en

[24] Annual report, 2019

[25] Romans 12:14-21; 1 Peter 2:12

[26] Romans 12:21

[27] https://www.powergrp.co.za/about.html

[28] In 2019

[29] www.unashamedlyethical.com

[30] Proverbs 8

[31] Proverbs 1:8

[32] Ecclesiastes 1 and 5:8-17

[33] For example, Proverbs 12:27; 13:4; 18:9; 19:5; 21:5

[34] Ecclesiastes 11:1-2

[35] *The Seven Qualities of Effective Leaders*, Steven Covey, business contact, 2010.

Chapter 9: Creating Well-Being

[1] Isaiah 9:7; 11: 4-5; 54:14

[2] Revelation 19:8

[3] https://www.bbc.com/news/business-34324772

[4] http://news.bbc.co.uk/2/hi/7720404.stm

[5] Proverbs 29:12

[6] https://en.wikipedia.org/wiki/Corporate_social_responsibility

[7] Earnings before interest and taxes

[8] https://www.bosch.com/company/our-figures/

[9] https://www.bosch-stiftung.de/and/what-we-do

[10] https://www.focusplaza-foundation.nl/

[11] Unique selling point

[12] https://www.bambook.org/

[13] https://annualreport.ingka.com/who-we-are/

[14] In this book, I will not explain every aspect of the economics of mutuality but will just give you a broad idea to help you as a Jerusalem entrepreneur understand the concept and how contributing to well-being is anchored in this model. More information is available at the website eom.org and in the book *Completing Capitalism.*

[15] https://economicsofmutuality.com/what-is-eom

[16] Bruno Roche and Jay Jakub, *Completing Capitalism*, Berrett-Koehler Publishers, 2017.

[17] Matthew 25:31-46

[18] Matthew 25:31-46

[19] https://kenniskaarten.hetgroenebrein.nl/en/knowledge-map-circular-economy/what-is-the-definition-a-circular-economy/

[20] Revelation 11:18

[21] Romans 8:20-21

[22] Genesis 3:17-19

[23] Romans 8:19-22

[24] Hosea 4:1-3

[25] Matthew 6:24; Luke 16:9-13

[26] Hebrews 13:5, 1 Timothy 6: 9-10, 17-18

[27] https://www.doubleharvest.nl/

Chapter 10: Motivation and Meaning

[1] The last attribute from our definition of a Christian Jerusalem entrepreneur.

[2] In order to emphasize the transcendent and irrevocable otherness of the other person, Levinas deliberately writes "the Other" repeatedly with a capital letter.

[3] Genesis 1:27, Genesis 2:20-23

[4] The Harvard Gazette, April 11, 2017, https://news.harvard.edu/gazette/story/2017/04/over-nearly-80-years-harvard-study-has-been-showing-how-to-live-a-healthy-and-happy-life/

[5] Otto de Bruijne in Onderweg.

[6] 1 Corinthians 13:1-3

[7] Hebrews 12:2

Chapter 11: Ownership

[1] Psalm 24:1, Psalm 89:12, 1 Corinthians 10:26

[2] Leviticus 25:23

[3] Psalm 50:10-12

[4] Haggai 2:8

[5] 1 Corinthians 6:20

[6] Titus 2:14

[7] Luke 14:33

[8] Luke 18:18-23

[9] Ecclesiastes 5:19

[10] This version of the story is an adaptation of the story from the Dutch book: *Ik wens je genoeg (part 2)*, from Anders Invest, March 2019

[11] Deuteronomy 28:11-13; Ecclesiastes 5:18

[12] Deuteronomy 31:20

[13] Deuteronomy 8:18-19

[14] Also, see 2 Chronicles 29:12

[15] Isaiah 60:4-13

[16] Matthew 25:14-30

[17] Luke 18:26-27

[18] Luke 18:29-30

Chapter 12: Division of Roles

[1] Acts 9:4

[2] Matthew 4:4

[3] Mark 1:35-38; Luke 22:39-46

[4] Luke 5:16

[5] Psalm 37:5; Isaiah 28:23; Luke 11:5-13; Hebrews 4:16

[6] Acts 17:27

[7] Luke 11:9-12; Luke 18:1-7

[8] Acts 2:6

[9] Acts 17:27; Matthew 7:7

[10] Proverbs 16:3, 20

[11] John 20:11b and 20-23

[12] John 15:9

[13] Genesis 1:26

[14] Deuteronomy 8:2; Exodus 15:30

[15] Exodus 13:17-18; Hebrews 12:7

[16] Micah 6:8

[17] Matthew 22:37-38

[18] Proverbs 16:9; 20:24

[19] John 10:10

[20] Romans 8:28

[21] Chr. A. Schwarz, Natural Church Development, ChurchSmart Resources, 1996.

Chapter 13: Love in Business

[1] These words and the concept of love are discussed extensively in the chapter Two Cities: Babylon and Jerusalem, under the section "Loving Relations: Connection and Service."

[2] Matthew 22:36-40

[3] Matthew 22:37-40

[4] https://hbr.org/2014/10/the-value-of-keeping-the-right-customers

[5] https://www.annexcloud.com/blog/39-referral-marketing-statistics-that-will-make-you-want-to-start-a-raf-program-tomorrow/

Chapter 14: Connection Within Business

[1] From Paul CH. Donders, out of his book Resilience, de Barbara, 2015.

[2] https://and.wikipedia.org/wiki/Volatility,_uncertainty,_complexity_and_ambiguity

[3] https://www.ncbi.nlm.nih.gov/pmc/articles/PMC3116346/

[4] https://www.ibm.com/watson/health/

[5] https://www.c12group.com/blog/gift-of-covid-19-constraints/?utm_content=132498496&utm_medium=social&utm_source=linkedin&hss_channel=lcp-128414

[6] Bruno Roche and Jay Jakub, *Completing Capitalism*, Berrett-Koehler Publishers, 2017

[7] See Chapter 3, "Who We Are," as well as Chapters 5–7.

[8] Chuck Blakeman, *Making Money Is Killing Your Business*, Crankset Publishing, 2010

[9] Frederic Laloux, Reinventing Organizations, Laloux (Frederic), 2016

[10] https://www.mt.nl/leadership/frederic-laloux-maak-organisaties-als-de-natuur-daar-is-ook-niemand-de-baas/88525

[11] https://www.buurtzorgnederland.com/

[12] Frederic Laloux, Reinventing Organizations, Laloux (Frederic), 2016

Chapter 15: Earning Models

[1] 2 Timothy 2:2

[2] Paul Donders and Chris Sommer, *Meesterschap*, de Barbaar 2012.

[3] 2 Corinthians 6:14